PENNSYLVANIA'S
Historic Places

Purchased   7-11-90   at Daniel Boones
Boyhood home   near Birdsboro PA

Read:

PENNSYLVANIA'S
Historic Places

TEXT BY RUTH HOOVER SEITZ
PHOTOGRAPHY BY BLAIR SEITZ

Good Books

Intercourse, PA 17534

in cooperation with
Pennsylvania Historical and Museum Commission

Acknowledgments

Detail photograph of the United States Brig *Niagara* taken from the painting *The Battle of Lake Erie: Commodore Perry in the U.S. Brig Niagara Breaking the British Line of Battle, Lake Erie, September 10, 1813* by Julian O. Davidson, 1885/1887. Oil on canvas, 36″ × 84″. Photograph by D. James Dee. Courtesy of Lynn S. Beman, Beman Galleries, 114 Main Street, Nyack, New York 10960.

Commodore Oliver Hazard Perry, portrait by Gilbert Stuart and Jane Stuart, gift of Florence Scott Libbey. Oil on wood panel, 26⅝″ × 21¾″. Courtesy of the Toledo Museum of Art, Toledo, Ohio.

Black-and-white photos courtesy of the Pennsylvania Historical and Museum Commission, except where noted.

Thanks to Michael J. O'Malley III of the Pennsylvania Historical and Museum Commission for assistance with the text.

Special thanks to Douglas H. West of the Commission for editorial, layout and production advice.

Design by Beth Oberholtzer.

PENNSYLVANIA'S HISTORIC PLACES

Library of Congress Cataloging-in-Publication Data

Seitz, Ruth Hoover.
  Pennsylvania's historic places / text by Ruth
Hoover Seitz ; photography by Blair Seitz.
    p. cm.
  Bibliography: p.
  ISBN 0-934672-75-X : $29.95. — ISBN
0-934672-76-8 (pbk.) : $19.95
    1. Historical sites — Pennsylvania — Guide-
books.   2. Historical museums — Pennsylvania
— Guide-books.   3. Pennsylvania-Description
and travel — 1981 — Guide-books. I. Seitz,
Blair. II. Title.
F150.S45   1989   89-7491
917.4804'43 — dc20   CIP

Printed by Printer Industria Gráfica sa
Barcelona   D.L.B.: 14362-1989

Contents

Introduction   6

Pennsbury Manor   12

Morton Homestead   18

Graeme Park   22

Hope Lodge   26

Washington Crossing Historic Park   30

Pottsgrove Manor   36

Brandywine Battlefield   40

Valley Forge   44

Independence National Historical Park   50

Hopewell Furnace   58

Daniel Boone Homestead   62

Landis Valley Museum   66

Ephrata Cloister   74

Railroad Museum of Pennsylvania   82

Museum of Anthracite Mining   88

Eckley Miners' Village   92

Pennsylvania Anthracite Heritage Museum   98

Scranton Iron Furnaces   102

Conrad Weiser Homestead   106

Cornwall Iron Furnace   110

Gettysburg National Military Park   114

The State Museum of Pennsylvania   122

Pennsylvania Lumber Museum   128

Joseph Priestley House   132

Pennsylvania Military Museum   136

Somerset Historical Center   140

Bushy Run Battlefield   146

Fort Pitt   150

Flagship Niagara   154

Drake Well Museum   158

Old Economy Village   164

Map and Addresses   172

Readings and Sources   174

About the Author   176

About the Photographer   176

Introduction

Pennsylvania began in 1681 when King Charles II granted a charter to the colony's founder and first proprietor, William Penn, a member of the Religious Society of Friends (Quakers). Inscribed in the founding documents were the principles of freedom of conscience, liberty and broad participation in government by which Penn intended that the province be governed.

The immigrants who crossed the Atlantic Ocean in search of freedoms espoused by Penn were not the first in the hemisphere, however. At least 12,000 years earlier, Ice Age families first crossed the Bering Strait from Alaska to Siberia to hunt their prey. Dispersed to the far corners of the hemisphere, native Americans had long been resident as hunters and farmers when the British king, with a presumption of authority, created Pennsylvania.

Indeed, Penn and those who followed him were not even the first Europeans in the area. The colonizers whom the Indians first welcomed to the Delaware Valley were supported by English, Dutch and Swedish trading companies. These firms were chartered by competing governments to exploit the natural resources of distant lands, conduct trade and sustain the enterprises through farming. Colonization was meant to profit the shareholders and gain a competitive edge among Europe's dynastic and national rivals.

Although the English and Dutch were the first to trade with the Lenni Lenape, a people they called the Delaware Indians, it was the New Sweden Company that settled the first colony in the Delaware Valley. Founded in 1638, the New Sweden colony extended from the present site of Philadelphia to New Castle, Delaware.

Most Swedes, however, could farm their own land at home and had little motivation to risk a fearsome voyage to the New World. As a result, many of the immigrants to the colony were actually Finns. They and the other settlers in New Sweden constructed the first log houses in colonial America. One such structure, known as the *Morton Homestead*, has long been attributed to the family of Morton Mortenson. The house still stands in Prospect Park.

From 1643 to 1653, the energetic and ambitious Johan Printz served as governor of New Sweden. Printz guarded the peace of his colony by taking care to compensate the Indians for their land. At the same time, he outbid the English and Dutch for the Indians' furs and began cultivation of tobacco for export. Even so, the colony was never really a success, and in 1655 it was seized by the Dutch. In 1664, it was taken over by the British.

The Dream of William Penn

Along with the aggressive pursuit of national interest, a zeal for reform spurred European colonization of North America. This was especially true among English visionaries, such as William Penn.

Pennsylvania's founder was born in London in 1644 to Margaret Penn and her 24-year-old husband, William, soon to be an admiral in the royal navy. England was in the midst of civil war between Charles I and Parliament. In hope of "a new heaven and a new earth," the biblically inspired voices of dissent had risen to demand thorough reform of the established church, government and society. After the king was beheaded in 1649, however, Parliament wearied of the austerities of the reformers. In 1660 it restored the throne to Charles's son, Charles II, and enacted penalties against a wide variety of religious dissenters.

In October of 1660, William entered Oxford University and began his association with nonconformists. His father, now Sir William, attempted to counteract their influence, but in time young William decided to join the Friends in their witness for peace, justice, equality and Christian simplicity. Thus he began, in spite of confrontations, arrests and trial, a long life of preaching and writing.

Politically, the younger Penn became an ardent champion of ordered liberty, religious freedom and limited, constitutional government. On returning from a visit to the New World, George Fox, a Quaker founder, proposed the establishment of a haven there for persecuted Friends. Seeking a profitable investment, Penn seized upon the idea and presented a plan to the king. It would be a "Holy Experiment," Penn said, "that an example and standard may be set up to the nations."

In his colony, Penn took the extraordinary step of welcoming *anyone* who believed in God, regardless of the immigrant's religious affiliation. To the traditional liberties of Englishmen, he added a further provision: "Government is free to the people under it . . . where the laws rule and the people are a party to them." In keeping with his Quaker beliefs, he required neither the bearing of arms nor the swearing of oaths. He took care to be just in transactions with the Indians. The punishment of crime, both public and private, was to be milder than provided by English law and was to be concerned with reform.

With a Quaker's concern for public virtue, the proprietor warned his citizens against greed, luxury and indifference to the poor, though he defended social distinctions resting on wealth and public service. How these standards received public expression is suggested in his plantation at *Pennsbury,* near Morrisville, begun in 1682 and reconstructed in the 1930s. The estate reflects the manners of a Quaker gentleman, as does *Hope Lodge,* a classical Georgian house erected in Whitemarsh by businessman Samuel Morris.

A prosperous gristmill owner who had many investments, Morris was active in public office and the Quaker meeting. At the time of his death in 1770, he was one of the last Quakers in Pennsylvania who was a slaveowner. Although many of the early settlers in the colony owned slaves, an anti-slavery movement soon developed in Pennsylvania. In 1688, a group of Quakers in Germantown made the first formal protest against slavery in the New World. In 1780, the Pennsylvania Assembly passed the first state law providing for the emancipation of slaves.

Freedom for African Americans did not mean full equality, however. In 1787, Richard Allen and Absalom Jones formed a Free African Society to oppose discrimination. In response to segregated seating in churches, Allen founded the African Methodist Episcopal Church in Philadelphia in 1794.

German Religious Communities

The search for freedom of worship drew many of the early immigrants to Pennsylvania. During the 17th century, Europe—and Germany especially—had been embroiled in war and divided by religious differences. A revival of Christian piety pointed to an era of reform and, in time, of greater freedom; however, religious reform often met strong resistance from both church and state when it embraced separation from the world, repudiation of state religion and refusal to fight or swear oaths. William Penn's assurance of freedom of worship was an attraction to members of many religious groups and initiated what

would become a major migration of German-speaking peoples to Pennsylvania.

Though by no means identical to one another, these sectarians shared a belief that Christianity had been submerged in priesthood, ritual and doctrine—that it had lost its fervor. Rejecting the enticements of a sinful age, they often looked to Christ's return and the start of a new age. Many of the faithful were attracted to charismatic leaders. During both the 18th and 19th centuries, the availability of land and freedom in Pennsylvania presented the opportunity for religious prophets and secular reformers to establish communities.

Among the German sectarians who carried their dreams to the land of Penn's experiment were members of the Ephrata community and the Harmony Society. Conrad Beissel founded the *Ephrata Cloister* in Lancaster County in 1732. George Rapp established the Harmony Society, which settled Harmony, Pennsylvania, then New Harmony, Indiana, and finally *Economy* (now Ambridge) in Beaver County in 1824. Though self-educated and of peasant origin, both Beissel and Rapp were men of compelling personality. Banned by the authorities in his homeland, Beissel sailed to Philadelphia in 1720. Rapp, seeking a new country for his followers, sailed to the New World in 1803. Both of their communities adopted celibacy: the Harmonists as the bride awaiting Christ's return, and the Ephrata members to follow a daily discipline borrowed from the monastic tradition and rites of spiritual initiation. Both Ephrata and Economy prospered financially from agriculture, mills and manufacturing. In addition, both communities became known for their artistic accomplishments.

Inevitably, celibacy contributed to the ultimate dissolution of Ephrata and Economy decades after their founding. Peter Miller, a brother at the Ephrata Cloister for 61 years, assumed its leadership in 1768; in a letter to Benjamin Franklin he reflected, "We have no successors, and the genius of the Americans is bound another way." But the reforming impulse in frontier evangelism remained, and would be rekindled again and again, with profound personal and social effect, throughout America.

The Promise of Land

Convinced that country living was superior to life in the city, Pennsylvania's founder invited newcomers to share the bounty of a "good and fruitful land." The English and the Welsh, the first to accept Penn's offer, settled in a vast fertile triangle that extended from the southeast beyond the *Daniel Boone Homestead* in Berks County. Germans established roots in the rich soil that stretches for miles around the *Landis Valley Museum* in Lancaster County. Next came the Scotch-Irish, some of whom settled in the area near the *Somerset Historical Center.*

Although rich harvests made Pennsylvania the leading agricultural colony, the farmers' crops and livestock were used largely to feed and clothe their own families. Methods of farming were traditional; many farmed by the stages of the moon or by the signs of the zodiac. Although the German settlers manured their soil, others did nothing to replenish it. The American Philosophical Society, founded in Philadelphia in 1769, was the first group to promote science as the solution. Agriculture recovered—and even prospered—between 1790 and 1840, the period in which many of the impressive farmhouses and barns that still dot the countryside were built.

Nevertheless, farm equipment remained simple and had changed little up to the time of the Civil War, when economic conditions spurred the adoption of labor-saving machinery. As farming became more commercial and methods more scientific, productivity increased. Farms grew larger but became fewer in number, and land was put to other uses.

Growth of Industry

It was not only agriculture which gave Pennsylvania stature in the colonies. Rich in natural resources, skilled workers and available capital, Penn's commonwealth became the industrial heart of the United States.

Ironmaking was a good investment for Philadelphia merchants and gave steady employment to many in the labor force. In 1720, Thomas Rutter opened the first iron furnace at Colebrookdale. With it began Pennsylvania's leadership in heavy industry and the extraction of natural resources. With the colonial worker's modest wage surpassing that of Europeans, and with the market for implements, housewares and other conveniences growing, some 200 furnaces and forges were erected. Plants such as *Cornwall,* opened in 1742 by Peter Grubb, and *Hopewell,* begun in 1771 by Mark Bird, were built near abundant sources of ore

and wood. They created plantations generally comprising the furnace, the ironmaster's—or owner's—mansion, workers' cottages and the plantation store. Among those who rose to wealth and civic position through ownership of such furnaces was John Potts, who married Thomas Rutter's granddaughter Ruth and built stately *Pottsgrove Manor* at Pottstown in 1754.

Led by Pennsylvania, the American colonies smelted one-seventh of the world's iron. Charcoal-fueled furnaces such as Cornwall and Hopewell played a major role in helping the colonies to arm for the Revolution. However, the development of hot-blast furnaces fueled by anthracite, or hard coal, made it possible to produce better iron at less cost. Factories of this type, such as the *Scranton Iron Furnaces,* made the charcoal furnace obsolete by 1850. By the Civil War, Pennsylvania provided more than half the nation's anthracite-produced iron. Meanwhile, the conversion of bituminous, or soft, coal to coke began to fuel the production of steel. By 1880, Pennsylvania produced four-fifths of the nation's coke.

Mining, Oil and Lumber

The acceleration of industrial growth, particularly in coal and steel, attracted great waves of immigrants to Pennsylvania between the Civil War and World War I. These European peasants and Southern share-croppers, unable to sustain themselves and their families from the land, were of ethnic and religious groups largely new to Pennsylvania. Those who found work in the mines settled with their families in company-owned "patches" such as *Eckley* in Luzerne County. The anthracite region's economic and social history is examined by the *Pennsylvania Anthracite Heritage Museum* in Scranton, while mining processes and technologies are explored at the *Museum of Anthracite Mining* in Ashland, Schuylkill County.

In addition to its preeminence in coal, the principal fuel of economic growth, Pennsylvania was the leading source of petroleum, the miracle illuminant and lubricant of the industrial age. The *Drake Well Museum* near Titusville stands on the site of the world's first successful oil well.

For years Indians had collected oil from the surface of streams, and so had the settlers. But demand had begun to outrun the supply, so investors hired Edwin Drake to find a way to extract it in larger quantities. In August 1859, Drake's well began to produce about 20 barrels a day. Prospectors swarmed into the region, creating boomtowns. The railroad penetrated the region and in 1865 the first long-distance oil pipeline spanned the five miles from Pithole to Oil Creek. Within 20 years, the legendary entrepreneur John D. Rockefeller had maneuvered his way into virtual control of the industry in Pennsylvania.

Meanwhile, the commonwealth had eclipsed neighboring New York as the largest producer of timber. The majestic white pine was in greatest demand. It grew in abundance in such northern areas as Potter County, where the *Pennsylvania Lumber Museum* is located. Wood was essential to meet nearly all the needs of a growing nation—ships, wagons, carriages, houses, implements, household goods, containers and fuel. The harvest of hemlock, used in leather tanning and building construction, invigorated the Pennsylvania industry into the 20th century.

Transportation Network

Industrial growth increased the need for easier and faster means of transportation. In 1792 the Pennsylvania Assembly chartered the first privately owned toll road in the United States, between Philadelphia and Lancaster. By 1821 it had authorized 150 more. Because overland travel was slow, private interests turned to the building of canals. By 1834 Philadelphia and Pittsburgh had been linked by the Main Line of the state-owned Pennsylvania Canal.

Rail transport further increased speed and accessibility. In 1839 the Philadelphia and Reading Railroad was completed to Reading, and in 1852 the Pennsylvania Railroad crossed the mountains to Pittsburgh. With cities to serve, natural resources to extract and mountains to cross, Pennsylvania became a major force in railroading, from management to manufacturing. The railroad's extraordinary impact is reflected even in the Pennsylvania Constitution of 1873, articles of which attempted to restore integrity to the relationship of government and this politically powerful industry. At the *Railroad Museum of Pennsylvania* near Strasburg, rolling stock and other train memorabilia can be viewed.

Conflict and Compromise

The railroad's challenge to government was not the first political difficulty faced by Pennsylvania citizens and their public officials. Penn's plan of representative government, conducted in a spirit of harmony between the proprietor and the people, did not function as he had hoped. Under Pennsylvania's charter, which gave Penn ownership and ultimate authority, he empowered the elected Assembly only to approve or reject the laws proposed. The Assembly, however, quickly demanded greater authority, and was eventually conceded the right to initiate legislation.

Given the failure of settlers to pay the feudal rents owed on their lands, the attempts of the Assembly to tax the proprietor, and the Assembly's refusal to appropriate money for colonial defense, political conflict was understandable. After the founder's death, however, the long-standing dispute was unilaterally resolved in the Assembly's favor by the governor, Sir William Keith (the builder of a picturesque country retreat later known as *Graeme Park*). Angered by Keith's action, the Penn family dismissed him from his position.

Despite continuing disharmony and the apparent failure of the founder's dream, the spirit of democracy —brightened by the diversity of peoples and ideas and the absence of traditional barriers—became a permanent feature of life in Pennsylvania. There were, after all, contradictions which permitted practical solutions even as they tarnished the original plan. In the charter, King Charles II had appointed the pacifist Penn to be the "Captain-General" of his province. Moreover, after briefly losing the proprietorship, Penn had promised in 1694 to present London's requests for military assistance to the Council and Assembly. Normally, such requests were refused. The proprietor's sons, who succeeded him, discarded his pacifist theology, but the Assembly continued to reject pleas for a militia, in spite of growing British tensions with the French and native Americans. Finally in 1755, after France's claim to the Ohio Valley had ignited the French and Indian War, the Quakers of the Assembly acquiesed and passed a militia act.

Indian Relations

From the time of Pennsylvania's founding until the 1750s, the colony and local native Americans had maintained peaceful relations. In their first encounters with Europeans, the Indians in the Delaware Valley generously extended hospitality in the belief that the land and its creatures had been freely given to all by the Creator. For the colonists' part, the provincial government paid the native Americans for their lands and attempted to protect them from unscrupulous traders. Guided by Conrad Weiser, the frontier diplomat whose contributions are commemorated by the *Conrad Weiser Homestead* at Womelsdorf, the province created an alliance with the Iroquois. Under it, this tribe was to protect the colony from French ambitions and to control the Delawares and other Pennsylvania Indians. In time, however, the French awakened old Indian grievances, and the peace was irreparably shattered.

The object of French ambition was the Ohio Valley, the entrance to which was the Forks of the Ohio at what is now Pittsburgh. Until its abandonment in 1758, Fort Duquesne defended the Forks in the name of France. In 1761, the British completed Fort Pitt, a masonry and earth fortification many times the size of its predecessor. Only once was Fort Pitt called upon to resist an attack—during Pontiac's Rebellion in 1763, when the resentment of displaced Indian tribes boiled over into attacks on colonists in the West. The siege which the native Americans laid to the fort was raised by Colonel Henry Bouquet and his British and American troops in their victory on the *Bushy Run Battlefield* near Jeanette, Westmoreland County. *Fort Pitt Museum* in Point State Park depicts the conflict of British, French and Indian interests, as well as Pittsburgh's earliest years.

Pennsylvania and Revolution

Barely a decade after Pontiac's uprising and the official end to the French and Indian War, Pennsylvania was again involved in a military conflict—the Revolution against Britain. In the War of Independence, Pennsylvania played a crucial role, manufacturing arms, lending money, raising troops, provisioning soldiers and providing leadership.

In the years leading up to the Revolution, Pennsylvania had been deeply divided—not so much over Parliamentary taxation, colonial trade and Western settlement, but over the questions of independence and war. To confer on the crisis, representatives from Pennsylvania and its sister colonies met at Philadelphia in two Continental congresses, the first in 1774 at Carpenters Hall and the second convened in 1775 at the Pennsylvania State House, now Independence Hall. At the second gathering, the delegates agreed

upon the means of resistance to the Crown, declared their independence of British authority and formed a government of the United States. The halls where these meetings took place are among the venerable buildings at *Independence National Historical Park.*

Resistance to Parliament ripened in 1775 into war. To the British soldiers, who had a long military tradition, the ill-prepared Americans appeared of little account. Their confidence seemed justified when General Howe drove the rebels from New York in the late summer and fall of 1776. However, George Washington's audacity in crossing the Delaware River in winter from what is known as *Washington Crossing Historic Park* and driving the enemy from Trenton and Princeton, New Jersey, revealed the difficulty of compelling obedience in an overseas war.

In late summer of 1777, Howe won a major victory on the *Brandywine Battlefield.* He sent 15,000 troops from New York, landing them at the head of Chesapeake Bay on August 25. To prepare for the first encounter, Washington deployed his Army on the east bank of Brandywine Creek to intercept Howe's northward advance. On September 11, Howe sent a small detachment to divert Washington at Chadds Ford, while a large column crossed upstream and surprised the American command on its right. Even though the patriots acquitted themselves well, they were outnumbered and outmaneuvered. At day's end they retreated to Chester.

After the battle at Brandywine, Howe entered Germantown on September 25 and prepared to occupy Philadelphia. Washington decided to strike again. However, mistakes and misfortunes led to a costly American defeat. Washington's army endured a difficult winter at *Valley Forge* (1777–78), but a new spirit and regimen were instilled under the tutelage of the Prussian Captain Friedrich von Steuben. In June, when the troops broke camp, they were better prepared to fight.

Another crucial development that spring was the entry of France into the war on the side of the rebels. This helped to tilt the Revolution in favor of the Continental forces. In 1781, combined forces from the United States and France won a decisive victory over the army of General Cornwallis at Yorktown, Virginia.

Among those of stature in Britain who expressed public sympathy for the American Revolution was Joseph Priestley, the English theologian and pioneer in chemistry who discovered oxygen in 1774. Priestley was an ordained minister in the dissenting tradition and a champion of political and religious liberty. His support for the French Revolution, as well as the American cause, made him the subject of intense opposition. In 1794, he left England with his wife, Mary, and three of their children and settled in the Pennsylvania village of Northumberland, five days' journey from Philadelphia. There they built their comfortable white frame house. Now known as the *Joseph Priestley House,* it is a lasting tribute to his place in the democratic enlightenment that shaped the Declaration of Independence and the U.S. Constitution.

War of 1812

Despite the triumph at Yorktown and the Treaty of Paris in 1783, it seemed to many people that the United States was still in thrall to the interests of foreign powers. In 1803, France and Britain were again at war, resorting to the weapon of the commercial blockade. The United States, active in shipbuilding and maritime trade, was divided as to which combatant it should support. To many, the Royal Navy's impressment of British — and even American — seamen from U.S. ships, along with Britain's assistance to the Indians of the Northwest Territory, was an affront to American sovereignty.

In 1812, Congress declared war on Britain. Pennsylvania supported the U.S. cause with men and money. However, the state's poorly trained militia shared in the failure to clear the enemy from the Canadian frontier. After a series of early British victories, the Navy was ordered to challenge the British on the Great Lakes. Doing so required the construction of six wooden warships in Erie, an isolated frontier village with few men and little material. Yet Commodore Oliver Hazard Perry and the others assigned to the task completed construction in just 10 months. The reconstructed *Flagship Niagara* at Erie was the second vessel from which Perry commanded the U.S. fleet in its victory at the Battle of Lake Erie on September 10, 1813.

A Nation Preserved

Half a century later, the Civil War climaxed the persistent conflict between the agricultural economy of the South and the more industrialized North, enflamed by the moral question of slavery. Gettysburg, a small town in south central Pennsylvania, was the scene of one of the most important battles of the war. In three bloody days of fighting, Union soldiers repelled the Confederate forces of General Robert E. Lee that were attempting to provision the rebel army, disrupt rail transportation and undermine the North's commitment to the war. One-third of the men who fought in the battle were Pennsylvanians. The valor of Union and Confederate soldiers alike is commemorated at *Gettysburg National Military Park.*

Since the Civil War, many thousands of Pennsylvanians have participated in military conflicts around the world. Their efforts, along with those of soldiers in the 18th and early 19th centuries, are depicted at the *Pennsylvania Military Museum* at Boalsburg.

Today's Pennsylvania is a place of rich variety, composed of cities, farms and forests, quiet villages and sprawling suburbs. The "Holy Experiment" of Penn has grown into a commonwealth shared by people of every race, faith and country of origin. The diversity of Pennsylvania's landscape and people is depicted in *The State Museum of Pennsylania* in Harrisburg. From ages of geological and biological formation, through the progress of aboriginal and native cultures, to the social, cultural, technological and military experiences of the past three centuries, the museum presents a graphic portrait of a region.

Out of the social idealism and religious reform upon which Pennsylvania was founded have emerged democratic government and economic leadership. The pages that follow provide a window on Pennsylvania's — and America's — past and on some of the people and events that shaped a nation.

—Harold L. Myers, Pennsylvania Historical and Museum Commission, December 1988

Pennsbury Manor

Moving slowly with the tide, William Penn's boat traveled north on the Delaware River late in 1682. With each passing mile, Penn's excitement must have grown. For years he had dreamed of a "Holy Experiment"—a place where Quakers, such as himself, and other persecuted dissenters could live and worship freely. Now, with a grant of 26 million acres from King Charles II of England, the vision was about to become reality.

Much had already happened since Penn's arrival in the New World in late October. He had met the Indian chiefs to whom he had sent a letter a year earlier, stating his "great love and regard" for them. He had arranged for a meeting with Lord Baltimore to iron out a border dispute between "Pennsylvania," as the new colony was called, and the neighboring colony of Maryland.

Between the Delaware and Schuylkill rivers, he had inspected the tiny village of Philadelphia. Only 10 houses stood near the wharf, but others would soon rise along a wide avenue

and crossing streets. The town's harbor and location along two watercourses pleased Penn.

He was overjoyed with the country's "soil, air, water, seasons and produce." Natural life seemed plentiful—wild fowl, fish, trees, grapes, fur-bearing animals. More deeply than ever, he believed what he had said about the colony before he left England: "I am firm in my faith that the Lord will prosper it."

As he continued upriver, his eyes may have roamed the banks, thick with oaks, chestnuts and hickories. Along the river's edge grew bayberry shrubs with

waxy berries. Up ahead Penn spotted the site that his deputy William Markham had selected for the mansion. This crook of land on a bend in the river held a commanding view of the countryside. Again, Penn was pleased.

This would be his retreat from the responsibilities of governing the colony. Most of his time would be spent in Philadelphia, seeing to endless political and administrative details. But here, on these 8,400 acres some 26 miles north of the city, he could reflect on his life and on God's natural bounty. In his early years of marriage, he had preferred the English countryside to London. Now, he had acquired a similar setting in the New World for himself and his children. He wrote his wife,

Keys (above) unlock the front entrance of William Penn's reconstructed mansion (opposite page).

Gulielma: "Of cities and towns of concourse beware; . . . a country life and estate I like best for my children."

Penn ordered that construction of the house begin without delay and appointed James Harrison as overseer in 1684. After returning to England in August of that year, Penn wrote many letters to him and later caretakers about the maintenance of the grounds.

A dedicated conservationist, Penn delighted in nurturing the soil and planting trees. He

(Upper left) A Thomas Moore Ipswich lantern clock with one hand sits in the parlor. (Upper right) The master bedchamber is adorned with wool damask hangings, an oak blanket chest (c. 1680) and a table set with pewter chocolate pot and mugs.

instructed Harrison to get soot from Philadelphia to fertilize the ground on the estate and to start an orchard. Penn's second gardener brought 4,000 saplings to the property and also grew cherry, plum and peach trees from seeds.

The trees were maturing when Penn returned to his colony in 1699 — this time with his second wife, Hannah, his grown daughter, Letitia, and his

25-year-old personal secretary, James Logan. After a winter in Philadelphia, where the Penns welcomed a new son, John, the family spent the summer of 1700 at Pennsbury.

Because the manor was barely accessible by road, the Penns traveled there by boat. A stone path led them up the steps from the riverbank to the front door and main foyer of the three-story house. The chimneys damaged during a thunderstorm had been repaired. Horses grazed in a fenced meadow, and cows, pigs and sheep roamed free. A kitchen garden with parsnips, artichokes and herbs grew beside the red brick dwelling.

Food was prepared by the domestic staff in a kitchen detached from the house; the Penns, like other people of their social class, preferred to keep the living area free of cooking smells. At a table set with pewter, china and damask linens, the family dined on mutton, beef, smoked shad, Indian corn and imported claret. Fruits and nuts came from the orchards —a special interest of William, now in his fifties.

In anticipation of picking sweet cherries, Penn himself planted several English redhearts. He recommended interspersing apple trees with peach; by the time the apple foliage was spreading, the short-lived peaches would die out. Guests had long enjoyed the estate's apples, figs, apricots and pears. The gentleman owner was so skillful at drying fruit that he

The 17th century manor house, bakehouse and brewhouse at Pennsbury, the country estate planned by William Penn as his retreat from Philadelphia.

shared his recipe with his mother-in-law. To his first wife he had written, ". . . agriculture is especially in my eye; let my children be husbandmen and housewives . . ."

Along with his fruit trees, Penn took special pride in "the court"—a formal flower garden in front of the house. A fence kept the garden private, while a retaining wall ensured that it would stay level and protected it in case of flood.

But political storms, rather than natural ones, threatened Penn in 1701. Economic problems and political maneuvering forced him to hurry back to London to persuade the Crown not to strip him of his proprietorship. His wife and family went with him. Before their departure, Delaware Indians from nearly 100 miles around canoed to Pennsbury as a sign of their continued goodwill. One sachem explained that his people did not keep agreements with their heads—he touched his three times—but in their hearts. After an exchange of gifts, the Indians bade farewell to a man who had kept his promise made in 1681— to win their "love and friendship by a kind, just and peaceable life."

With great sadness, Penn left

his estate. He tried to manage it by letter, entreating Logan, "Forget not poor Pennsbury." Slowly, however, the manor deteriorated along with the financial situation of its owner. Penn died in 1718, and his descendants sold the property in 1792.

Visitors never stopped coming to the estate, however. Throughout the 18th and 19th centuries, Pennsylvanians and others came to honor the commonwealth's founder. Today

Pennsbury stands as a monument to this creative, committed man who spent his life, health and fortune to build Pennsylvania.

What to See Today

William Penn's estate, Pennsbury Manor, lies at the end of a mile-long lane near Levittown in Bucks County. Reconstructed on the original foundations in the 1930s, the elegant brick and clapboard manor house is surrounded by outbuildings and

Sun lights the joiner's shop, equipped with a historically accurate wheel lathe. Penn planned his estate to be a self-sufficient plantation.

gardens. Guided tours provide an introduction to Penn and the property.

Pennsbury has the largest exhibit of 17th century furnishings in Pennsylvania. Items of pewter, ceramics, wood and wicker are displayed, along with period and reproduction textiles.

Penn's love of nature is reflected in the estate's present 43 acres. Horses roam a fenced meadow, sheep graze and Red Devon cattle chew their cud. Pea and guinea fowl cackle and strut about the many trees on the property.

Flowers popular in the 17th century brighten the property. Two striking spring flowers are the red valerian and Rembrandt tulip. Cardinal flowers, originally transplanted from the woods at Penn's request, bloom scarlet in the summer.

Pennsbury's garden grows the same varieties of vegetables as it did 300 years ago, including corn salad, Romaine lettuce, carrots, asparagus, artichokes and podded peas. Parsnips and cabbages, which were winter staples during Penn's time, are also grown.

Walking the grounds of Pennsbury Manor, and touring the rooms arranged as the Penns may have enjoyed them, help the visitor to understand why Pennsylvania's founder called the estate a "better place than any I've lived at."

Near the stone barn, an Arabian gelding pastures with a mare of a breed that grazed at the manor during Penn's time.

Morton Homestead

Crowing from his crate, the cock announced a new day inside the log cabin of the Mortenson family. Morton, the head of this 17th century immigrant household, crawled out from a bearskin blanket and punched his bed of straw ticking. He pulled on elkskin trousers and slid his feet into the wooden shoes he had carved after his leather pair wore out.

It was barely dawn along the Delaware River, but Mortenson wanted to finish threshing before breakfast. The door opposite his corner fireplace led to a storehouse made of logs, where sheaves of rye hung on stands. Mortenson expertly swung his hand-blade, knocking off the grains.

New Sweden, the first European settlement in what is now Pennsylvania, was Morton's third homeland. Born in Finland, he moved to central Sweden to clear forests by the slash and burn method. After Sweden outlawed forest burning, he took passage with his family on a ship bound for the New World.

The Mortensons' expedition was one of 12 organized by the New Sweden Company under Queen Christina to trade with the Lenape Indians and establish a colony. Neither poor nor craving religious freedom, most Swedes had no desire to settle in North America. Some, perhaps Mortenson, volunteered for the sake of adventure. But many who went on the expeditions, which began in 1638, were army deserters or petty criminals who preferred life in a foreign wilderness to imprisonment.

Certainly, a person needed to have strong determination—or nothing left to lose—in order to risk the journey at sea. Packed together in cramped quarters with coarse food and putrid water, people shared what one voyager called "violent and contagious diseases." The open deck offered little comfort. The sun "could have fried a herring," a traveler recalled. "When the roll was called in the morning, there would be three, six, eight or nine corpses."

Grateful to have survived the trip, Mortenson began to pay off his passage by working on the company's tobacco plantation. During those years as an indentured servant, he took notice of the resources along the Delaware, then called the South River. Now, as a free man, he was co-owner of a homestead

(Left) A boardstol, or table chair, beneath a spice cabinet and knackebrod, a rye cracker. (Opposite page) The Swedes and Finns who came to Pennsylvania in the mid-17th century made many items out of wood.

bordering Darby Creek, which fed the river.

This morning, after finishing breakfast with his wife and children, he lifted the latchstring of his door and stepped outside. Mist hugged the tall grasses along the freshwater marshland, still noisy with croaking frogs and buzzing insects. Mortenson let himself into a rowboat and pushed off to spear fish and check the traps he had set for beaver and otter.

Opportunities to trade the pelts were limited. For the past several years, no ships had arrived from Sweden. Practical to the point of crudeness, Mortenson was used to doing without European luxuries, but the family needed salt and cloth. They could manage without iron because they owned a copper pot and Morton was skilled at whittling with his knife. Hunched over in the light of the gable window, he often carved spoons, cups and saucers. Sometimes he made buckets out of wooden bands.

Not given to homesickness, Mortenson missed the spruce trees of Scandinavia less for their beauty than for their usefulness: without a whisk pared from the top leader of the evergreen, his wife had trouble getting the lumps out of maize porridge.

Tonight's supper consisted of a pot of the steaming corn cereal. Family members spooned the thickened sauce into individual bowls already filled with milk. This treasured liquid came from the goat each evening.

When dusk shadowed the log walls chinked with moss and clay, Mortenson lit splinter-sticks that he had cut from pine branches. Sitting by the fire, he smoked the pipe he had carved and drank wine he had fermented from sour grapes that grew wild.

Occasionally he purchased beer at New Gothenburg, the colony's headquarters and fort on Tinicum Island. Johan Printz, the stout and forceful governor, had built a brewery and grist mill, but lacked supplies and settlers to carry out all the instructions given him by the queen.

New Gothenburg, where the Printz family lived in a mansion that had glass windows and china dishes, was also Mortenson's destination for court proceedings. People going to the creek to travel often trampled his crops. He and his neighbors had filed a complaint.

Occasionally, Mortenson worshipped at the Lutheran church the settlers had built at Tinicum. He found additional social life among his neighbors, many of whom were also of Finnish stock.

A wood-pegged door and original straw mortar at the Morton Homestead. The house was built by a Scandinavian family before the time of William Penn.

After years of neglect by its mother country, New Sweden was absorbed by the Dutch and then by the English. Before Mortenson's death in 1706, it had become part of Pennsylvania.

Born and raised under English rule, Mortenson's grandson John changed his surname to Morton. The founder's great-grandson John Morton, Jr., signed the Declaration of Independence in 1776.

Much had occurred since the Finnish and Swedish immigrants built a community with seeds, skins and wood. But their re-sourcefulness provided a solid foundation on which to construct William Penn's colony, even to launch an independent nation.

What to See Today

A restored log cabin stands along Darby Creek in Prospect Park in Delaware County. Built in the Scandinavian tradition, the house is typical of those in the very first colony in Pennsylvania. Its 17th century wood furnishings remind visitors of the scarcity of metal in New Sweden and provide a sense of the daily life of the early settlers.

Built of logs and mortar, the Morton Homestead illustrates construction techniques introduced by the Swedes and Finns, the first Europeans to settle in Pennsylvania.

Graeme Park

Pennsylvania at the dawn of the 18th century was a place for dreamers. In William Penn's proprietary colony, it seemed that hard work and a little luck could make anything possible. Yet, as the residents of Graeme Park discovered, fortunes could fall as easily as they climbed. From 1721, when its stone walls rose along Park Creek, this country manor near Horsham was the scene of both joy and heartbreak, of dreams realized and crumpled.

A yearning for land may have lured Sir William Keith to seek another position in the colonies after Queen Anne died in 1714 and he lost his appointment as Surveyor-General for the Southern District of the Americas. In 1717, William Penn appointed him Governor of Pennsylvania in one of the last official acts before Penn's death.

With great energy, Keith settled his family in the Governor's Mansion in Philadelphia and plunged into his responsibilities. His performance at two Indian conferences proved his skill as a diplomat, and he

gained praise for his trade policies.

In 1721 Keith obtained 1,700 acres at Horsham—in a manner suspect of impropriety, the Pennsylvania Assembly later charged. Keith intended to build a malthouse on the site to make beer and whiskey. Though his brewing plans were never fully realized, he erected several structures on the estate he called Fountain Low. A three-story stone building with a gambrel roof and two unusual double chimneys served as a summer retreat.

Believing, erroneously, that the Penn family was about to lose its proprietorship of the colony, Sir William made decisions offending his benefactors. Dismissed in 1726, he sailed alone back to England two years later and died in debtors' prison. He was Pennsylvania's only titled governor.

Keith's wife, Lady Anne, remained in the colony after her husband's departure and spent some time in the unfinished stone house at Fountain Low. A 1726 inventory of the Keith family possessions included an abundance of furnishings, china and fine silver, as well as eight adult slaves, nine horses, 29 cows, 31 sheep and 20 hogs. But Lady Anne gradually lost her wealth and died forsaken in Philadelphia.

(Above) The early 18th century mansion at Graeme Park includes advanced features for its time, such as paneled indoor shutters and windows with pulleys and sash counterweights.

Graeme Park, built by Sir William Keith in the 1720s, is the only surviving residence of a colonial Pennsylvania governor.

Ann Diggs, Lady Anne's daughter from a prior marriage, married Dr. Thomas Graeme. A friend of the Keith family, Graeme bought 835 acres of Fountain Low in 1739. A respected physician who handled quarantine at the port, he dreamed of making the estate a retreat from Philadelphia's summer heat and disease. Graeme planted crops and raised livestock for income, in the style of English country manors. In addition, he developed a park with grass under tall trees "as a piece of beauty and ornament to a dwelling," he wrote John Penn.

Besides beautifying the grounds of what he now called Graeme Park, the doctor decorated the mansion's interior. Carpenters installed molded wall paneling from floor to ceiling. The fireplaces were adorned with King of Prussia marble and tiles from Holland.

Paneled indoor shutters completed the windows that Keith had equipped with pulleys and sash counterweights for raising and lowering. For conve-

(Above) Chinese geese swim in a spring-fed creek in front of the mansion at Graeme Park in Montgomery County.

nience, Graeme altered some walls, setting up an office for himself on the main floor and two rooms on the third for his nine children.

The youngest member of the family, Elizabeth, was a poet and brilliant conversationalist. After a broken romance with Benjamin Franklin's son William, she broadened her education in Europe, moving in literary circles. When her mother died suddenly, she returned home to manage her father's household.

In the spring of 1772, Elizabeth married Henry Hugh Ferguson, a Scotsman who was 10 years younger. The wedding took place without the knowl-

edge of her 83-year-old father, who disapproved of the match. When she tripped over a gravestone as she left the church, someone remarked that this could be a bad omen.

A few months later at Graeme Park, Elizabeth had decided to tell her father the unwelcome news. From her second-floor bedchamber, she watched him come up the gravel path from his morning walk. She wrote in her diary how it happened that he never found out about the marriage: "As he reached the tenant-house, near the gate, he fell and died. Had I told him the day before, as I thought of doing, I should have reproached myself for his death and gone crazy."

As the only surviving child, Elizabeth inherited Graeme Park and moved into the mansion with Henry. Quite happy for several years, Elizabeth drew on the idyllic setting for the poems she published. But political differences drove a wedge into the marriage. With revolution brewing, Ferguson remained loyal to England. He sailed there, deserting her for two years. Then, in 1777, he reappeared in Philadelphia with the British and served as Commissary of Prisoners during the city's occupation.

Elizabeth visited Henry with passes from the Americans, but she refused to follow him as a Tory, preferring to endure suspicion and isolation at Graeme Park. During that time, Anthony Wayne's brigade encamped at the manor and

Elizabeth confirmed her allegiance to the rebels. But after the war, when her husband returned to England with the British, the new government seized Graeme Park as the property of a traitor. After three years of legal battles, Elizabeth proved that the property was hers before her marriage to Ferguson. But her loneliness remained. Using her pen name, Laura, she wrote of her desire to woo her husband back:

> Then might I hope to touch each string
>
> Which glows in Henry's breast;
>
> Soon waft him home on love's soft wing,
>
> And be like Delia blest.

Elizabeth sold Graeme Park in 1791, not knowing whether her husband was living or dead.

Subsequent owners preserved its 18th century features in a setting reminiscent of an English estate. After 1821, no one lived in the mansion. Instead of installing modern plumbing or electric light, the owners maintained the house in its original condition as a memorial to the dreams it had stirred.

What to See Today

The mansion at Graeme Park features elaborate chimneys, a Swedish gambrel roof and fieldstone masonry. Intact and unaltered, the interior wainscoting shows the woodworking skills of colonial Pennsylvanians. Yellow pine paneling in high Georgian design adorns the parlor. A false door in the room matches the entrance on the other side of the marble fireplace and provides symmetry.

Outside, visitors can picnic near a spring-fed creek that flows through the 42-acre property. The estate remains as it was described by Dr. Thomas Graeme two centuries ago: "a park . . . quite different from any I have seen here or elsewhere."

Among the parlor features added by Dr. Thomas Graeme after 1739 were wall paneling and a false door to balance the real one. The paint is original.

Hope Lodge

Eighteenth century business-man Samuel Morris pored over his ledger book. His investments included a gristmill, a brewery, a storehouse and improvements on two ships and a wharf. In addition to these properties, Morris owned Whitemarsh Estate, where he built his palatial home on a 150-acre tract. He could

easily walk from the mansion to one of his businesses, Farmar's Mill, which sold flours, lime, molasses and such miscellaneous products as cedar shingles.

Many of the grains for the mill came from Morris's farm. Besides raising the crops, laborers dug lime, made casks and carted goods. Often, Morris obtained goods and services without money, through exchanges. A meticulous manager, he recorded these barter arrangements as well as outright purchases and sales.

To pay a debt one December, his farm hand George Ogleby taught Robert Hughes "the cooper business," according to Morris's records. When Joseph Stern did carpentry work, Morris paid with grain products and lumber. To another laborer who drove his team for a year, Morris disbursed cash, grain, linen and a sheep.

People settled their accounts at Farmar's Mill in similar fash-ion. John Collister made and mended shoes, and Robert Rennalds dug a cellar. A certain Mr. Miller recruited his wife to

work for Morris! Such arrange-ments helped the bachelor businessman to run his house-hold.

Morris's mansion was de-signed for his servants' conve-nience as well as his own. His housekeeper's chamber led through a small passageway from the parlor. Her fireplace could keep tea warm for his guests, perhaps Quakers from Gwynedd Monthly Meeting, of which he was an active member. She had access to the pantry, to the winter kitchen and well, and to the underground storage rooms — one for cured meats, another for root crops and a dairy cellar with standing water for cooling.

Each of the six main rooms of the house had built-in closet space. Such innovative design touches may have been sug-gested by Edmund Wooley, a

(Far left) Underground storage room with original brick flooring. Cured meats were kept here.

Samuel Morris, a prominent Quaker businessman, built his mansion in the style of the early Georgian period.

respected architect and master carpenter of Independence Hall, who came to the mill to buy horse fodder in 1743 during the months that Morris was constructing his home.

In addition to its practicality—a value of Morris's Quaker faith—the mansion was undeniably grand. Like other houses of the early Georgian period, the front facade featured carefully balanced windows on four levels, from the cellar to the third-floor dormers. Inside lay a wide hall with arched doorways. People may have waited here during his tenure as Assessor for Philadelphia County and Justice of the Peace.

Samuel Morris died a prosperous man in 1770. He left bequests for several Quaker meetings, for a free school in the area and for his slave, Joseph Nettle, to train "in a trade such as he may like." By this time the Philadelphia Yearly Meeting, of which he was a member, strongly condemned slavery. Morris was one of the last Quakers owning slaves in Pennsylvania. In 1780 the Pennsylvania Assembly passed the Abolition Act, making the state the first to emancipate slaves.

For a century and a half, Morris's house passed through the hands of owners who respected its integrity. James Horatio Watmough, a cousin in the family that gave the Hope Diamond its name, received the house as a wedding present in 1784 and renamed it Hope Lodge.

In 1922, William and Alice Degn purchased the house in order to save it from demolition by an expanding limestone quarry. History buffs and antique collectors, the Degns used Hope Lodge as a summer dwelling only, to avoid defacing the antique cellars with a furnace.

The building provided a perfect showcase for their 18th and 19th century artifacts during the Colonial Revival. Mrs. Degn enthusiastically visited sales and auctions, packing her mansion museum with Chinese porcelain, Hepplewhite furniture, draperies, candles and the like—far more furnishings than Morris could have imagined. She delighted in hosting civic organizations at the house and showing them its features.

By this time, the story of the original owner had largely been lost. It would take the architectural research of the 1980s and the discovery of Morris's ledger

(Left) Alice and William Degn redecorated the dining room during the Colonial Revival. (Above) Gardens brighten path to side entrance of the mansion. (Opposite page) Arched doorway frames the mid-18th century parlor.

to uncover the rich past of Hope Lodge.

What to See Today

Built around 1750, Hope Lodge is a striking example of 18th century Georgian architecture. A rare blind niche and door hood emphasize the symmetry of the front brick facade. The interior features a central hall with arched doorways that are graced by pilasters and pediments.

A striking arch hides the main stairway, so the corridor can flow the length of the house. The work-efficient kitchens and cellars suggest that the home was planned to accomodate more than one person.

It is unknown why Samuel Morris, who never married, had such a house built. According to local lore, he was engaged to a woman in England during the building's construction. When the dwelling was finished, he is said to have remarked, "Now the sty is completed, and all it needs is the sow." According to the story, his comment reached his fiancee, who broke the engagement.

Today the decor of Hope Lodge reflects the style of two eras—the simple but refined furnishings of a frugal Quaker gentleman of the mid-18th century and the eclectic room arrangements of two antique collectors and preservationists of

the early 20th century. On the main floor, the rooms on the north side depict the Morris era. The south side represents how Alice and William Degn decorated the house during the Colonial Revival. In addition to touring the house, visitors can walk in the gardens, under the arbor or across Bethlehem Pike to Mather's Mill, a quaint structure built on the site of Morris's Farmar's Mill.

Seeing the furnishings and workplace of this colonial businessman alongside the artifacts of a couple trying to recapture his era provides a fascinating view, not only of the 18th century but of how history is preserved and interpreted.

Washington Crossing Historic Park

December 1776. General George Washington weighed the military options for his Continental Army. Should he wait for an offensive from the British and their German mercenaries, gloating together on the New Jersey side of the Delaware River, or could he dare a surprise attack?

The enemy could not cross by water, because Washington had ordered Daniel Bray to collect all boats up and down the river, tying them on the Pennsylvania shore. But a freeze would enable the British to bring their artillery and men across the ice.

The weather seemed headed in that direction. A heavy snow had fallen and bitter winds whipped through the Delaware Valley.

Washington's men were hardly equipped for camping in these conditions. They had left supplies behind as they retreated. No tents. Many had no shoes and could only "lace their feet in the hide of freshly killed beef," one general wrote.

The kitchen of the Thompson-Neely house. Washington's generals gathered in the house to plan the dramatic crossing of the Delaware.

In the shadow of Bowman's Hill there were few farmers who could feed the revolutionaries. Fewer still were willing. Many colonists had lost hope that the British could be defeated. Rural people preferred the silver money of the king to the paper the revolutionaries paid for goods.

Washington felt keenly the desperateness of his situation. His men grew weaker each hour they waited. Yet how could they move without fresh supplies or recruits?

Behind them lay many defeats. At Long Island, Washington's untrained 8,000 had been routed by 20,000 of Britain's finest. And the American general recalled how hesitation had cost his army Fort Washington and nearly 3,000 men.

He vowed not to repeat the error. He would not let Philadelphia be taken. He would lead an offensive across the Delaware!

He must not wait. The tour of duty for many of his soliders would be finished at the end of the year. His officers said that very few would re-enlist.

Washington gave the orders to his generals headquartered in five homes near the hill. They would cross and attack at dawn while the British were sleeping off their Christmas festivities.

Several generals argued that the move was suicidal. The morale of the men was low. They were worn, hungry and home-sick, huddling over fires near Pidcock Creek and eating raw flour from Thompson's mill. Some of the soldiers were dying of pneumonia. One of the rooms at the nearby Thompson-Neeley house had been turned into a makeshift hospital.

General Stirling, whose headquarters were in the house,

(Left) Eighteenth century clock at McConkey's Ferry Inn, where Washington waited before his crossing of the Delaware on Christmas night, 1776. (Above) Reproduction of Washington's letter to General John Cadwalader at Bristol, in which Washington states his determination to cross the river.

Crossing. When he heard that General Cadwalader's men could not give support further south, he wrote the General, "If you can do nothing real, at least create as large a diversion as possible."

Washington knew that the battle—perhaps even the war—would depend on the 2,400 men who would board vessels 100 yards north of the ferry. But he shrugged off any sense of gloom, maintaining the determination that naturally showed in his jaw. In a recent letter he had written, ". . . under a full persuasion of the justice of our cause, I cannot entertain an idea that it would finally sink. . . ."

At 4 p.m. the soldiers began loading their artillery, despite snow, bitter winds and floating chunks of ice in the river. The men pushed 18 field cannons onto the boats. As the driving snow turned to sleet, the wild-eyed horses balked at getting on board.

It was four in the morning before the entire party safely

supported the plan. As Surveyor-General and Washington's second in command, he had prepared maps of New Jersey. He had hiked to the top of Bowman's Hill to evaluate possible attack routes.

Stirling believed that the plan could catch the British off guard.

The rebels would cross in heavy, flat-bottomed Durham boats, which usually carried iron ore. Each would be rowed by eight oarsmen. An island would hide the activity from enemy eyes.

On Christmas Day, Washington awaited last-minute reports at the inn at McConkey's Ferry

(Above) An exact copy of Emanuel Leutze's oil painting Washington Crossing the Delaware, *shown here in detail, hangs in the Visitors Center.*

reached the New Jersey shore. A freezing rain glazed the trail. Sunrise would come at 7:23, and there were miles to march to Trenton.

All the leaders set their watches to Washington's, and two columns broke off from his. Later, one sent word that its wet muskets couldn't be fired. "Use the bayonet," the General replied. "The town must be taken."

It was. Holiday frivolity and the frigid weather had weakened British alertness. All flanks of the colonists followed their orders, capturing more than 900 soldiers. When the last regiment reported, Washington said, "This is a glorious day for our country."

What to See Today

More than two centuries later, the drama of the crossing is portrayed in the oil painting

Washington Crossing the Delaware by Emanuel Leutze. A full-size copy of the 21 × 12 foot canvas hangs in the Visitors Center of the Washington Crossing Historic Park at the site of the actual event.

Within the 500-acre park are several sites important to the

attack, which rekindled support for the colonial army.

Inside stone-walled McConkey's Ferry Inn, built in 1752, the 18th century is re-created through the use of historic tavern furnishings. An English-made clock on the wall would

Dessert is served in the dining room of Mahlon Taylor, a Quaker who lived beside his store near McConkey's ferry crossing in the 19th century.

have been useful to travelers waiting for the ferry, as they shared news over card games and cider.

Several miles north along River Road, a tower marks the top of Bowman's Hill, the tree-covered rise that General Stirling used for observation.

Inside the Thompson-Neeley House hangs a portrait of Robert Thompson Neeley, who would have been seven years old in 1776, when his family left to stay with relatives for three weeks while Washington's officers occupied their home. The cozy hearthside room was undoubtedly the setting for planning the crossing.

On a shady knoll overlooking the Delaware are stones marking the resting places of early patriots who died of disease that fateful December. The only identified grave is that of Captain James Moore of New York, who died on Christmas Day at the age of 24.

The park, which encompasses two sections along the Delaware,

also interprets the life of a town a century after the crossing. In the riverbank hamlet of Taylorsville near the inn are houses and shops from the early 19th century. Beside his general store lived Mahlon Taylor, a prominent Quaker citizen.

Along with reminders of the past, Washington Crossing Historic Park offers many opportunities for hiking and enjoying nature. The Bowman's Hill Wildflower Preserve is part of a natural memorial to the soldiers who died during the Revolution. Its trails, open year round, meander through 100 acres.

The botanical garden in the Preserve is the only wildflower garden in the country accredited by the American Association of Museums. The collection includes 750 species, all of them native to Pennsylvania. Among these are all seven azaleas native to the state. The marsh marigold, rare for Pennsylvania, appears in April. Bluebells cover the floodplain in springtime, and cardinal flowers lure hummingbirds in summer. Butterfly weed blooms in July.

Far from traffic and the noise of modern life, the Preserve offers birdsong, a babbling creek and the hum of insects—sounds as welcome for people today as the news of victory was to citizens of a new nation.

(Left) Onions and drying spices hang in the kitchen of the Thompson-Neely house. (Center above) Turk's-cap lily is one of the 750 species within the botanical collection of Bowman's Hill Wildflower Preserve. (Right above) Downy phlox grows in the preserve, part of a natural memorial to the soldiers who died in the area during the Revolution.

Pottsgrove Manor

Wealth. Empires. Intermarriages. In the 18th century, these not only characterized the royal families of Europe but the iron families of colonial Pennsylvania. Like rulers of tiny nations, these capitalists from the Schuylkill Valley built dynasties around their forges and furnaces and put up ever more elaborate mansions. Marriages between families blended fortunes and expertise.

In one such union, John Potts, who had learned ironmaking from his father, Thomas, married Ruth Savage, the granddaughter of Thomas Rutter who founded Pennsylvania's iron industry at Colebrookdale in 1720. The couple's wedding in 1734 took place at Coventry, a palatial home built by Samuel Nutt—Ruth's stepfather and owner of the furnace that first cast Benjamin Franklin's stove.

While Ruth was born into wealth, John's family had only acquired it gradually through his father's ironmaking and business abilities. Expert management of a furnace and its workers enabled the ironmaster who rented it to pay the owners and himself shares of the output as agreed in the lease. During 27 years as ironmaster of Colebrookdale

Paneled woodwork in the parlor of ironmaster John Potts shows his wealth and refined taste.

Furnace, Thomas Potts bought shares of the production and land as they became available. In addition, he appointed John founder, the position in which Thomas had started.

John bought one-third share of Pine Forge, where he could turn his iron share from Colebrookdale into more valuable bar iron. From that point, he acquired interests in forges and furnaces in a way almost too complex to fathom. Through his mother-in-law, who had been born into one iron family and married into two others, John secured a link to all the major ironworks in the Schuylkill Valley.

After building Pottsgrove Furnace and buying a thousand acres nearby, John and Ruth decided to build a large home to accommodate their expanding family—one that would total 13 children. In 1752, John chose a site overlooking the Schuylkill River, within view of the forge. At the same time, he laid out

(Above) Artist's rendering of Pottsgrove, built in early Georgian style in the 1750s. A later owner added Federal touches to the house.

Pottstown, the first town in Montgomery County.

With the keen sense of planning that he brought to his investments, John took two years to build his family a country manor. His wealth enabled him to build substantially. All four stories had windows, and the fieldstone walls were two feet wide. Inside the house were handsome corner cupboards and windows with sash pulleys and counterweights, as well as simple but fine wainscoting and mouldings. People came from 30 miles away to admire Potts's home.

Modern as could be, the house matched the stature of the family that owned it. According to family tradition, George Washington visited during the Revolution. Several of John's children contributed heavily to the patriot cause—Samuel as a

munitions maker and Jonathan as a doctor. John's eldest son, Thomas, raised, armed and equipped a battalion at his own expense.

While his wealth and family connections gained him fame, John Potts apparently was admired for his character as well. When he died in 1768, an obituary described him as "a gentleman of unblemished honor and integrity."

What to See Today

An impressive early Georgian-style mansion, Pottsgrove Manor stands overlooking the Schuylkill River, near Manatawny Creek in Pottstown, Montgomery County. The front entrance of the house opens into a wide central hall. Corner cupboards and window seats built into four rooms, as well as fireplaces decorated with paneled chimney breasts, show the elegant tastes of the original owner, John Potts. An elaborate, banistered stairway leads to the family bedrooms on the second and third floors. These rooms had no access to the servants' quarters on the same floors.

One of the family bedrooms shows how a later owner introduced Federal touches to the house. The room features fine marbelizing of the paint on the overmantle, door panels, corner cupboard and window shutters.

Pottsgrove Manor is furnished with 18th century antiques. Pieces are similar to those listed in a 1768 inventory of Potts' belongings, made at the time of his death. Paint colors match the original ones.

In addition to the interior of the house, a formal boxwood garden reflects the wealth of a successful 18th century ironmaster. In John Potts's world, financial rewards came from ironmaking skill, managerial ability and marrying well. Potts combined all three.

East end of the mansion of John and Ruth Potts. The substantial walls and advanced design of the house reflected the stature of the family that built it.

Brandywine Battlefield

As Chester County farmers cut their harvest at summer's end in 1777, they worried that this growing season might be their last. Talk at the mill said that the Revolution was headed for the Brandywine Valley.

British General William Howe had landed 15,000 troops at the northern end of Chesapeake Bay and was marching toward Philadelphia. George Washington's rebels were marching south to stop them.

The thought of a battle in their peaceful valley left the locals shocked and divided. Many were Quakers and objected to war of any kind. Many more were loyalists, who welcomed the British but feared the devastation that combat would bring. Still others supported the fight for independence but trembled at its cost.

Many residents fled the area, after hiding their valuables and newly threshed grain. The farmers who stayed watched 14,000 colonial soldiers crowd the roadways, their columns spilling onto the fields. Heavy cannon carriages and caissons

dug deep into mud left by heavy rains.

On September 9, the troops camped on the east bank of Brandywine Creek while General Washington set up headquarters in a house rented from Benjamin Ring, a wealthy Quaker farmer. Washington's new aide, Major General Lafayette of France, took lodging in the next farmhouse, owned by Gideon Gilpin.

During a meeting with his generals and other officers, probably including Lafayette,

Washington agonized over strategy. The gently rolling countryside offered no points high enough to survey the surrounding area. He had to rely on residents to pinpoint the location of fords where Brandywine Creek could be crossed.

General John Sullivan warned that the enemy might turn north before crossing the stream, coming around the colonists' right flank instead of attacking from the front. The British had used this tactic effectively in their victory at Long Island.

Washington disagreed. He and the other generals believed that the British would cross the creek before it forked and that there was no need to guard it further north.

Still, conflicting intelligence reports troubled Washington as

(Above) Quiet woods stand where Washington's army unsuccessfully fought the British. (Opposite page) Sycamore frames the Gideon Gilpin house, Lafayette's headquarters.

his army prepared its defenses. Were the British and Hessians advancing in one column or two? Where would Howe strike?

As Washington puzzled, his soldiers dug in on the neat 200-acre farms along the valley. Residents watched in dismay as soldiers tore up rail fences for firewood, grazed their horses at will and chopped down trees to line up artillery. The paper money paid for chickens and grain could not compensate for the losses that occurred before the fighting even began.

On September 10, the British made their move. General Howe ordered General Wilhelm von Knyphausen and several regiments to attack the revolutionary forces at Chadds Ford, as Washington had expected.

But the rebels were not prepared for the rest of his plan. Under cover of a dense ground fog the following morning, Howe himself led a larger column north. James Galloway, a loyalist who knew the area well, led Howe across fords north of the fork. Quickly, the company advanced toward the rebels' right flank.

Throughout the morning, Washington received contradictory word from his scouts. To make matters worse, he confused the names and locations of the fords. Not until two o'clock did he realize the seriousness of his plight. The British were surrounding him!

Washington ordered several contingents to meet Howe and General Charles Cornwallis, now near Birmingham Meetinghouse. The American commander put Anthony Wayne in charge of the forces facing Knyphausen at Chadds Ford.

In both areas, fighting raged, described by a British officer as "a most infernal fire of cannon and musquetry." At five o'clock, noise from the battle could be heard at Reading, 35 miles away. Three- and four-pound shells

splintered branches and plowed up the ground. Grapeshot stripped leaves from the trees as though it were autumn.

The colonials fought valiantly but could not hold back the enemy. Gradually, the rebel generals withdrew their divisions, retreating to Chester throughout the night.

Because of heavy losses, Howe did not pursue them. Washington pondered his men's courage and his own faulty strategy.

While the colonials regrouped and sent some of their wounded to the Ephrata Cloister, the victors destroyed what the battle and their enemies had not. They plundered the farms of people who had aided Washington, such as Gilpin and Ring. They bayoneted bedclothes, scattering

Cannon fire from the battle left branches in splinters and plowed up the ground. It took years for the Brandywine Valley to recover.

(Left) Interior of the Gideon Gilpin house features a document box (c. 1728) and iron and wooden candlestick owned by the family. (Below) The sun rises on Brandywine Battlefield in present-day Delaware County.

the feathers over the barnyard while their horses ate corn that was drying in the fields.

Elsewhere, the British ate chickens and pigs and stole grain. They strewed bits of furniture in fields and fireplaces. "There was no restraint," said Joseph Townsend, who had to move away because of his losses.

Gilpin faced destitution. He lost 10 milk cows, one yoke of oxen, 48 sheep, 12 tons of hay and 230 bushels of wheat. To provide for his six young children, he opened a tavern in his home. Selling liquor cost him his Quaker membership for eight years.

In 1782, at the request of the Pennsylvania legislature, 379 residents of Chester County filed claims for reparations. One farmer who received compensation in Continental currency said its real value was only 17 cents.

It took many years until productivity in the Brandywine Valley returned to prewar levels. Military defeat was only one of the losses suffered at Brandywine, the first battle of the Revolution fought on Pennsylvania soil.

What to See Today

Interpretive exhibits in the stone Visitor's Center introduce the people and locations of the Battle of Brandywine in 1777. A tour of the restored Gideon Gilpin House shows Chester County furnishings typical of a local family before this Revolutionary battle. Sycamore trees shade the property as they did when General Lafayette stayed here with the Gilpin family.

The reconstructed Benjamin Ring House, where Washington had his headquarters, reflects the lifestyle of a prosperous Quaker farmer and miller.

In addition to seeing these houses, visitors to the 50-acre site can take a self-guided driving tour of the battle routes of both armies. The tour explains one of the costliest defeats in the war for independence.

Valley Forge

Thoughts of the home he had left, battles past and challenges still to come must have flashed through the mind of George Washington as he watched his troops settle in at Valley Forge in December of 1777. It was almost Christmas. A year and a half after the Declaration of Independence, the revolution was still alive. The Continental Army had 12,000 men—more than four times the number with which he had launched the desperate crossing of the Delaware just 12 months before.

Yet all was not well. The winter had only begun, and the men were already short of food and clothing. Supplies were uncertain; a mutiny was not out of the question. The British were 18 miles away in Philadelphia, in far more comfortable circumstances. It was, he must have feared, to be a difficult wait until spring.

In some respects, the winter through which Washington and his army lived was less brutal than that of patriotic myth. The soldiers did not leave bloody footprints in the snow, although exposure and malnourishment caused illness. At one point, almost 4,000 troops were unable to report for duty, because they needed clothing and shoes; yet the camp bustled with the activity of the oversized town that it was.

With a pioneer mindset, each soldier put himself to whatever task needed doing. Using axes, the men in each regiment slashed trees to build rows of log huts. To construct a fireplace inside, they collected fieldstone or overpacked lathe with mud. Burning green wood smoked the only room, a windowless home for a dozen men. In their bunks padded with straw, soldiers who

Huts of Muhlenberg's Brigade are reconstructed according to the specifications that Washington gave his troops.

This defensive position protected the encampment against a possible southern attack from the British who occupied Philadelphia.

were ill writhed in discomfort. Vermin also lived in the straw, and bones cast aside from meals mounted in corners.

Outside, men in tattered clothing worked in various details. Some slowly dug fortifications to protect the camp in case of attack. Others set off with a cart—and paper money—to round up food. Because most of the horses had died for lack of fodder, one soldier pulled a cart of firewood while his companions pushed from the rear.

In one regiment that had not received beef for four days, several men baked "firecake" from flour mixed with water. From the brigade hospital, where the more seriously ill men were lodged, moans could be heard. Several wagons churned through the muddy snow to take typhus and smallpox victims to Ephrata to be nursed by German Baptists. Another smallpox sufferer, huddled in straw, left for the hospital at Yellow Springs.

Near a commissary, several men—one without shoes— unloaded barrels of flour from Lancaster. In an enclosure, cattle

(Above) The National Memorial Arch, built in 1917 by an act of Congress, commemorates the "patience and fidelity" of the Continental soldiers.

bawled. The stench from the waste of previous butcherings rose with the odor of horse carcasses—called "intolerable" by General Washington in one of his clean-up orders.

The General, based in the home of a miller named Isaac Potts, sympathized with his troops. Aware that his army needed time to recuperate, Washington resisted calls from Congress for an attack on the British. He established three markets to enable his soldiers to buy necessities from local ven-

dors and gave financial rewards as a way of increasing morale. When hut-building began, he gave a $12 prize for the first finished structure in each regiment. In addition, he offered $100 to the officer or enlisted man who could solve the problem of covering the camp's roofs. Orders called for the roofs to be tight, and some men were using their tents—which they would need again in the spring.

A general who kept his ear bent toward his men, Washington must have heard their ironic humor about shortages. The soldiers said many of their meals consisted of "a leg of nothing and no turnips." At one social event, only guests wearing a tattered piece of clothing were admitted.

For their part, British loyalists joked that the Army would always keep the Continental Congress well supplied with rags for making paper money.

What caused the soldiers' hardships? The wheels of the fledgling colonial government turned slowly and inefficiently. Congress failed to allocate transport money for the encampment, so supply units were frustrated by a lack of wagons and wagoners. For months the Quartermaster General, responsible to supply the Army's physical needs, underestimated the volume of supplies required for thousands of troops. He did not realize that the 10,000 barrels of flour sent by Mark Bird, the

ironmaster at Hopewell, would last for two months and not the whole winter. He ordered piecemeal and in a panic, never calculating how much had to be ordered to give each man his necessary rations.

Supplies dribbled in throughout the winter, but it wasn't until Major General Nathanael Greene became Quartermaster in March that the amount and variety of

provisions improved. Spring also brought fresh fish, as Pennsylvanians demonstrated how to catch shad that were swimming up the Schuylkill to spawn.

By this time, the voice of a forceful new officer was ringing from the brigade parades. Bringing high recommendations from Benjamin Franklin in France, Frederick William Augustus von Steuben appeared at Valley Forge in February to retrain the troops in strategies from the famed Prussian army. Washington assigned Von Steuben to organize a uniform system of drills. Until this time, the 60 some infantry regiments from 11

(Left) At Artillery Park, General Henry Knox oversaw the repair of weapons during the encampment. (Above) One of the huts near Artillery Park at Valley Forge.

states had used a confusing array of British, French and Prussian drills.

Von Steuben worked passionately, writing drill regulations at night. His secretary, Pierre Duponceau, translated them from French to English. Von Steuben himself trained a demonstration brigade, barking orders and expletives in a mixture of languages. Then he saw to it that his manual of arms was taught to the rest of the troops.

Von Steuben reorganized platoon columns, standardized their marching pace and taught them to keep step without drum-beats. He taught the patriot army to use bayonets for more than skewering meat and improved the soldiers' personal hygiene and appearance. Ragged enlistees appeared washed and shaven, and began to look and feel like trained soldiers. Von Steuben delighted in how quickly the men responded. Within two months, confidence emanated from an Army that had been determined but casually organized.

Another important foreigner in the camp was General Louis Duportail of France. As Chief of Engineers, Duportail drew maps of the Army's winter quarters, located where the Schuylkill River and numerous ridges formed natural barriers. These safeguarded the encampment, which in turn protected the breadbasket of southeastern Pennsylvania.

Word that the French had recognized American independence—a goal long sought by Franklin—reached the Army in the spring. After Washington reviewed the bri-

General Washington made his headquarters in the house of Isaac Potts, a local miller.

made to tour General George Washington's headquarters and the lodging of Brigadier General James Varnum, near the site where Frederick von Steuben from Prussia conducted drills.

Roads, bike paths and horse trails traverse the park. Visitors can follow a self-guided tour or explore the 3,000-acre facility on their own. Along the way, they can pause at reconstructed huts similar to those used by the Continental soldiers. Some of these structures follow Washington's specifications; others, based on archaeological findings, show that the General's orders were not followed by every original builder.

Four redoubts and Artillery Park show Washington's concern about fortification against the British, who were occupying Philadelphia. Like the National Memorial Arch, erected at Valley Forge in 1917 by an act of Congress, the defenses stand in tribute to the "patience and fidelity" of the Continental soldiers.

gades in their new formations, a *feu de joie* of musketry moved through the ranks, followed by cheers.

The celebration was a fitting climax to a long winter of hardships. An assortment of state regiments had solidified into a trained natural force. In June, Washington's men gave the British a difficult struggle at Monmouth, New Jersey, though neither side could claim victory. As additional troops came from France under the Treaty of Alliance, the British were forced to fight on many fronts. From 1778 on, they faced mounting defeats which eventually cost them the colonies.

What to See Today

In contrast to the constant activity during the six-month encampment in 1777–78, Valley Forge National Park today is tranquil, a verdant memorial to the endurance of the Continental Army. A stop at the Visitor Center introduces the encampment through a movie and exhibits. Arrangements can be

(Above) General James Varnum's quarters overlook the Grand Parade, where Inspector General Von Steuben drilled the American troops.

Independence National Historical Park

From all over the city, the crowd gathered at the Pennsylvania State House in Philadelphia. Since early in the morning —Monday, July 8, 1776— news had been spreading: Congress had drafted a resolution cutting the colonies' ties to Britain. The document would be read at noon.

Hundreds of people swarmed onto the lawn south of the assembly building, oblivious to the clatter of horses' hooves across cobblestone lanes and the stench of nearby Dock Creek, an open sewer. Laborers in leather and calico aprons sauntered from their sweaty work in warehouses and tanneries to listen from the shade of a tree. Merchants concerned about how trade would be affected drifted to the square from fashionable Second Street. Barefoot children played with pebbles, happy to be part of a crowd in front of Philadelphia's finest building.

Shortly after 12 o'clock, Colonel John Nixon strode through the Walnut Street entrance with a copy of the document. He clambered onto the wooden platform of Ritten-

house's Observatory a few feet above the crowd and read: "The unanimous declaration of the 13 United States of America." Governments are instituted to secure the rights of "life, liberty and the pursuit of happiness," the document said. But King George III had denied these rights and practiced "absolute tyranny." The Stamp and Townshend acts were examples of injustice, the declaration continued. Britain had not dealt with

the complaints raised two years earlier during the First Continental Congress—held just two blocks from here, at Carpenters' Hall. Instead, fighting had erupted between British soldiers and colonists at Lexington, Massachusetts. Now, the document said, the colonies had to separate themselves from their country of origin.

When Colonel Nixon finished, his dimple deepened and his jaw tightened. He and the other members of the Second Continental Congress had pledged their "lives, fortunes and sacred honor" in support of an armed rebellion. There could be no turning back.

The crowd's reaction was less subdued. Cheers rose, born of years of frustration with the

(Above) Weather vane atop Independence Hall, originally the Pennsylvania State House. (Opposite page) In this building, delegates signed the Declaration of Independence in 1776 and drafted a Constitution in 1787.

British. Bells pealed—no doubt including one that had hung in the State House tower and carried a biblical inscription, "Proclaim liberty throughout the land to all the inhabitants thereof." Later, this bell would become known as the Liberty Bell.

In the afternoon, the celebration continued with a parade and a 13-gun salute—one for each of the new states. A few Continental soldiers crept into the courtroom, adjacent to where the delegates had argued since May over how to respond to British "taxation without representation." The men tore down the king's coat of arms and dragged it to a huge bonfire.

Later, at the green-covered tables in the Assembly Room, delegates signed an engrossed parchment copy of the Declaration of Independence. Borrowing from the ideas of John Locke and other philosophers, Thomas

Jefferson had crafted the document's sentences in the stifling heat of his rented quarters on Market Street. John Adams edited the text—with too heavy a hand, Jefferson thought. Benjamin Franklin, Jefferson's colleague on the drafting committee, comforted the young Virginian from Franklin's endless stock of stories and aphorisms.

During most of 1777, the Congress again busied itself in the Assembly Room of the State House to draft the Articles of Confederation. This document defined the relationships between the states, which in many ways functioned like separate, allied nations rather than provinces of a united country. The need for a stronger central government became more apparent after the ratification of the Articles in 1781 and the end of the war in 1783. Different states used different currency. The

(Above) Period spectacles (1740–1790), case, quill pen, ballot box and pipe lie on a table in the Assembly Room. (Near right) This silver inkstand, designed by Philip Syng in 1752, was used by the delegates to sign the Constitution. (Far right) George Washington sat in this "rising sun" chair while he presided over the Constitutional Convention.

for the supremacy of the national government over the individual states. To many Americans, having just escaped the tyranny of king and parliament, the concentration of power in a few hands seemed ominous. So Madison proposed a three-part government with the power of each held in check by the others. Delegates voted by a six-to-one margin to create "a national government . . . consisting of a supreme Legislative, Executive and Judiciary."

Still to be determined was the form of these three branches. Franklin favored a one-house legislature—supposedly comparing a two-chambered legislative system to a two-headed

Confederation government could not tax, regulate interstate commerce or impose international tariffs. When states failed to pay their representatives, Congress was powerless to act. George Washington, who had led the revolutionary forces to victory, feared that the new nation was "fast verging to anarchy and confusion."

On May 25, 1787, delegates from 12 states—Rhode Island declined to send a representative—returned to Philadelphia to create a different governmental arrangement. In the Assembly Room, they met behind doors guarded by armed sentries. Many of the delegates were veterans of the war. The presence of Washington, who chaired the sessions, and 81-year-old Franklin helped to maintain order during the sometimes bitter debate.

Throughout a sweltering summer, "federalists" such as John Dickinson, James Madison and Alexander Hamilton argued

(Above) The Senate chamber in Congress Hall, restored as it appeared in the 1790s when Philadelphia was the capital of the new nation. Representation was one of the key issues at the Constitutional Convention. Delegates resolved the dispute by granting each state an equal number of votes in the upper house of the legislature, while allocating seats in the lower house on the basis of population.

(Above left) The clock tower on Independence Hall in Philadelphia. (Above right) An international symbol of freedom, the Liberty Bell draws visitors from around the nation and around the world.

snake with the heads venturing in opposite directions. Few agreed. The delegates created a Congress with two bodies, then resolved the explosive issue of representation through the Connecticut Compromise: each state would receive equal votes in the upper house, with seats in the lower house allocated on the basis of population.

Some of the Pennsylvania delegates—the quick-witted Gouverneur Morris and the cool-headed James Wilson—pushed

for a head of state elected directly by the people. Such radical democracy terrified many of the members, who believed it could lead to mob role. To allay these fears, the framers agreed that the President would be chosen by a group of electors from each state, who would be chosen by popular vote.

In just a few months, the delegates had completed a Constitution that set out broad principles in precise language. " 'Tis done," said Pennsylvania's

PENNSYLVANIA'S HISTORIC PLACES

Dr. Benjamin Rush. "We have become a nation." Franklin, whose eye had often been drawn during the proceedings to a sun carved on Washington's chair, proclaimed the illustration "a rising and not a setting sun."

Not everyone was delighted with the finished document, however. Several delegates refused to sign it, and Franklin himself admitted to certain reservations—though he added, "The older I grow, the more apt I am to doubt my own judgment. . . ." Several points stirred immediate public controversy. Opening with "We, the people of the United States," the preamble written by Morris ascribed the authority of the Constitution to the citizens and called the document itself "the supreme law of the land," superseding state laws. Congress had not asked the convention to limit the states' autonomy in such a drastic way. Virginians debated the Constitution hotly, with Patrick Henry calling the document a threat to freedom.

In response to public outcry, Madison drafted 12 amendments guaranteeing personal liberties. Ten of these became known as the Bill of Rights. They were formally proposed after the Constitution was ratified in 1789 and went into effect in 1791.

The Constitutional convention culminated the long public life of Franklin, whose home was less than three blocks from the site of the meeting. From his arrival in Philadelphia in 1723 as a poor 17-year-old, Franklin devoted his boundless energy to economic, scientific and political projects. He established a successful printing business, using

The Second Bank of the United States. Inside, a gallery displays portraits of the leaders who took part in the founding of a nation.

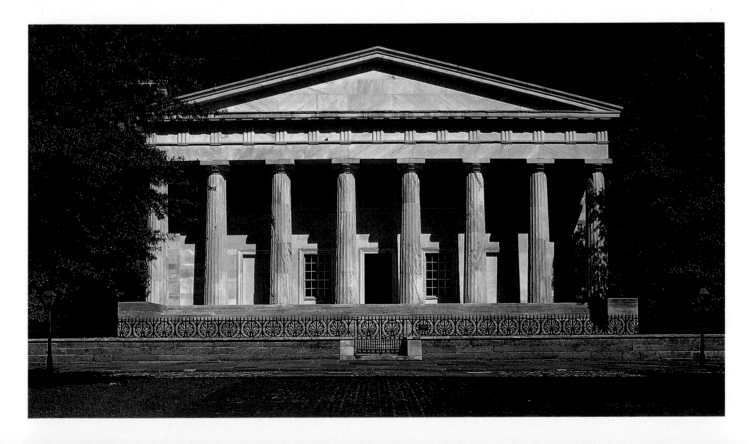

his presses to publish his own pointed sayings. In the 1730s he was the colonies' finest writer, and probably the one read with the most relish.

In middle age, the still-sprightly Franklin turned his attention to science and public service. He organized the American Philosophical Society and financed the Philadelphia Academy, which later became the University of Pennsylvania. Matters small and great fascinated him equally. To save time for his wife, Deborah, he invented a cradle that churned butter while she rocked the baby. He captured electricity from lightning, studied the Gulf Stream during

his voyages to Europe, was the first to plead with the Penns on behalf of the state assembly and served as emissary to France during the Revolution.

During his long absences, he and Deborah corresponded extensively on the style and furnishing of their house, situated in a courtyard off Market Street. After his wife's death, Franklin shared the house with his daughter Sally and her family. While he sat with friends under his mulberry tree during the last years of his life, Philadelphians enjoyed the fruits of his earlier endeavors. His legacy was everywhere—a lending library, a fire insurance company, street

An 18th century garden offers a quiet, restful stop in Independence Park, located in the heart of the city.

PENNSYLVANIA'S HISTORIC PLACES

lights and paving, police protection and an efficient postal system.

With his practical philosophy, Franklin epitomized the ideals of his newly-formed country. For a decade, beginning in 1790, the nation's three and a half million citizens were governed from Franklin's city. Philadelphia invited the Congress to meet in the new County Courthouse and the Supreme Court to hear cases in the new City Hall. The national treasury was headquartered in the First Bank of the United States.

In 1776, Philadelphia had been the birthplace of a nation. Now, as that country's first capital, the city would be the place in which the United States took its first, awkward steps toward adulthood.

What to See Today

With 12 acres of lawn in the heart of the city, as well as 31 acres of buildings and courtyards, Independence National Historical Park in Philadelphia attracts local residents and out-of-towners alike. At the Visitor Center, a film by John Huston introduces the dramatic events that took place here some 200 years ago. Guided tours of Independence Hall—the Pennsylvania State House in the 18th century—show the room in which the Declaration of Independence was signed and the Constitution framed. Flanking the building are Congress Hall, where the House of Representatives and Senate sat from 1790 to 1800, and the Old City Hall, where the U.S. Supreme Court deliberated from 1791 to 1800.

A map available in the Visitor Center gives directions to other places associated with the independence story, including Carpenters' Hall and the Liberty Bell Pavilion. Franklin Court, a memorial to Benjamin Franklin, includes an underground museum, a restored print shop and an architectural exhibit.

Several historic churches lie within the park: Christ Church, where many colonial leaders attended Episcopal services; the Free Quaker Meeting House; and St. Joseph's, the city's first Roman Catholic church. Tours of the Bishop White House and the reconstructed Graff House—where Thomas Jefferson drafted the Declaration of Independence—show the lifestyle of two Philadelphia familes during the 18th century. In addition, a walk through the portrait gallery in the Second Bank of the United States offers a chance to reflect on the early decision-makers of the nation—people who broke the bonds with Britain and forged a new and remarkable form of government.

(Above) Henry Inman's portrait of William Penn hangs in the gallery of the Second Bank of the United States. The doorway was moved here from an 18th century Philadelphia home.

Hopewell Furnace

The bell rang for the moulders at Hopewell Iron Furnace. Nathan Care grabbed his coat from a peg and took long strides to the casting shed. He hardly noticed the smoke or cinders rising from the furnace stack into the sky. Both the roar of the fire and the creak of the waterwheel were commonplace at this thriving industrial plantation on the border of Berks and Chester counties. The year was 1837.

With his eyes on the clay plug about to be broken, Care pulled on his gloves, grabbed his heavy ladle and waited in the casting pit with six other moulders. Perspiration trickled down his face. The long-handled dipper turned red-hot as he carried the molten iron to the open boxes, or "flasks," he had set up. He poured in a skillful, measured way—not too slowly and not too fast.

His was an ironmaking family. His father, Henry, rose through the ranks to become a "founder"—an expert in the mysteries of smelting. Henry had taught moulding to Nathan. In turn, Nathan would teach its secrets to his son.

Smoke and fumes from the cooling slag mixed with the

heavy dust of the casting shed. The odor of scorched sand rose to his nostrils as he poured several more ladles of liquid iron. His shoulders ached from the weight, but he carefully side-stepped tools and others' hot ladles. This was dangerous business.

When the task was over, Care set about preparing flasks for the next casting. To make the mould for the plates of an iron stove, he started by placing a follow board on his workbench as a base. Then he laid a mahogany pattern in the flask, which was packed with fine damp sand. The pattern would form the hot iron in the

shape of a stove part. On top of the sand, Care used a wedge to make a gate or opening for the liquid metal.

He liked the intricate stove patterns by Jacob Steffy, an itinerant carver. Some designs were biblical inscriptions or decorations such as hearts and flowers, all heavy enough to keep the tonnage up. That meant more income, because moulders were paid by the weight of finished castings. This year, Hopewell Furnace was moulding 138 types of stove designs, many for 10-piece stoves.

Crated in wooden cases, stove pieces were hauled by teamsters five miles to the canal landing for shipment by boat to Philadelphia, New York and Portsmouth. Some years, orders came from Baltimore, Wilmington and Boston, as well. In addition to stoves and Franklin fireplaces, the furnace produced sash weights, wagon irons and anvils, and plow castings and windmill irons for farms. Production had risen steadily in the

(Above) Side view of Hopewell Store, where furnace workers bought goods.

Casting flasks and follow boards lie outside the cast house, where iron products were moulded. The store, ironmaster's house and barn are visible from left to right in the background.

21 years since Clement Brooke became ironmaster.

At "the big house," as the workers referred to the ironmaster's mansion, Brooke's wife, Maria, spent much of her time hosting stove dealers. She received a $70-a-year allowance for this purpose. Located far from hotels, Hopewell offered accomodations for guests as well as living quarters for many workers. In the enlarged springhouse, servants did laundry, made soap and churned butter. Nathan Care could hear their laughter when he paused under a sycamore for a few minutes' relief from the heat.

Care and his co-workers agreed that life at Hopewell compared favorably with that at other Pennsylvania furnaces. The company store here was well stocked and offered fair prices. Casting fees did not come to moulders in the form of paychecks, but in credits to their individual accounts. Purchases from the store — for new clothes, housewares or tobacco — were deducted from the same account.

The food was good. Mrs. Brooke's staff served hearty meals with fresh baked goods during the 12-hour shifts. In addition, her husband was held in high regard by his employees.

In the cast house, moulders did the hot, dangerous work of pouring liquid metal into patterns for various iron products.

He appreciated good work and was willing to overlook an occasional slip, as when Henry Care joined his friends hunting and neglected a batch of molten iron. What a mess that made, as the liquid metal streamed across the floor of the casting shed!

In the past, the furnace typically went out of blast every 11 months or so for relining. Because of unusually high demand, however, Hopewell had now operated continuously for more than a year. Peak production boosted the need for ingredients for the furnace. Miners wrestled wagonloads of ore from nearby mines. Wood-cutters chopped 6,000 cords of wood a year for colliers to turn into charcoal. Fillers pushed carts of charcoal, iron ore and limestone across the bridge and fed the smelting around the clock.

To raise food for the workers, as well as to care for dozens of horses, required many acres of productive land. Apple and peach trees, a vineyard and large gardens grew fruit and produce for the company store and mansion kitchens.

For people with ambition, the busy furnace offered frequent opportunities to earn a little more money. Moulders paid laborers to grind charcoal dust for

lining a pattern, to haul sand and to clean castings. Along with jobs of this sort, workers had some chance for advancement. Nathan Care started as a moulder, became a founder and worked briefly as the furnace's manager.

When Mark Bird built Hopewell back in 1771, he could not have dreamed of the output or longevity of the furnace. Bird supplied cannon and shot to the Continental Army and shipped a thousand barrels of flour to the troops wintering at Valley Forge. His support for the revolution ruined him financially.

Hopewell faltered until the early 19th century, but became highly profitable from 1825 to 1844 as a manufacturer of stoveplates. In addition to good management by Brooke, the location of the furnace helped to make it a success. The surrounding area offered abundant raw materials. Charcoal, water power, ore and limestone remained in ready supply for more than a century.

As ironmaking technology changed, Hopewell's fortunes fell. The switch from charcoal to anthracite coal, and later coke, as the preferred furnace fuel— along with such innovations as the hot blast method— made Hopewell increasingly obsolete. The plant closed in 1883. At its peak, the furnace produced more than a thousand tons of pig iron and castings a year. Cast-iron stoves produced by its workers kept houses warm from Massachusetts to Delaware and helped to turn the United States into an industrial leader.

What to See Today

Hopewell Furnace, a 19th century ironmaking community, shows realistically arranged settings of its many workers, from ironmaster to servants. A tour explains life here at the peak of stoveplate production.

Visitors can enter the cast house with its L-shaped moulders' area. In the summer they can observe smelting and the disappearing art of flask-casting, by which moulders such

as Nathan Care made stove pieces.

Hopewell is one of two furnaces in the United States that have water-powered blast machinery. An indoor exhibit area introduces the steps of charcoal ironmaking and its role in U.S. industrialization.

The ironmaster's mansion, under a spread of tulip poplars and sycamores, includes furnishings for entertaining stove dealers. The nearby smokehouse, tenant houses, blacksmith shop and store illustrate Hopewell's self-sufficiency. Barnyard animals, living history demonstrations and a "pick-your-own" apple orchard with more than a dozen varieties bring quaintness to a site that once heaved with heat, noise and dirt.

(Above) The ironmaster's mansion, known to workers as "the big house." (Below left) After the castings cooled, moulders and their helpers cleaned them in Hopewell's cleaning shed. (Below right) Table is set in the moulders' kitchen on the ground floor of the mansion.

Daniel Boone Homestead

Three 18th century families stamped their imprint on this homestead near present-day Reading, but the property will be known longest for a young pioneer who grew up in its woods and fields.

Daniel Boone was born here in 1734, in the Oley Valley in Berks County. His father, an English-born Quaker, had purchased the site four years earlier. Though no longer wilderness, the area offered woods and fields dotted with tree stumps. The Schuylkill River was a mile away, and several streams wound through the 250-acre property. Over a spring that fed one of these, Squire Boone built a sturdy log house for his wife, Sarah, and their growing brood.

Daniel, the sixth child, seemed to have been born with one foot out of doors. Nothing pleased him more than roaming the forest and mastering the skills of a woodsman. He loved to observe the habits of game — deer, bears and the wild turkeys that were easily flushed out of the thickets of Flying Hill.

Beyond the mountains north of the Boone farm, Indian vil-

lages still clustered in the Tulpehocken and Ontelaunee Valleys. Boone's family befriended the native Americans, and on one occasion 25 Delawares visited his grandfather's nearby farm. Daniel himself met Indians while roving the hillsides along the Shawnee Path. From them he learned that deerskins taken in the spring gave the best leather and that beavers and otters trapped in winter had the thickest pelts. He imitated Indian ways of coping in the wild and soon could conceal his tracks as well as he could follow those of any animal.

When Daniel was 10 years old, his father bought 25 acres of pastureland four miles from the cabin, in order to build up his scraggly cow herd. Squire Boone had to mind his blacksmith shop and weaving, so Daniel and his mother took the job of watching the cows and making cheese during the grazing season.

Soon after his father gave him his first gun, a short rifle, Daniel went hunting and did not return. His father sent out a search party. After several anxious days, rising smoke in the woods led the group to a shelter spread with animal skins — all prepared by Daniel. Fresh meat roasted on the fire. Fearless and content, the young woodsman was reluctant to turn back to his livestock.

By the time Daniel was 15, he had hiked the blue-tinged hills that lined the valley and knew

(Above) Wooden plow (c. 1730) is among period implements at the homestead once owned by the family of frontiersman Daniel Boone.

the wetlands in the hollows. That year his father moved the family of 12 to North Carolina. The elder Boone split his property and sold the portion with the log cabin to William Maugridge, a relative who was of the Anglican faith.

The red shale in the earth may have reminded Maugridge of the land near Devonshire, England, where he and Squire Boone's family had grown up. What the homestead soil offered in memories, it seems to have lacked in productivity. Like Daniel's father, Maugridge did not prosper at farming.

He was better satisfied with the house. Enlarged by a stone addition, it took on English features. Some of these were probably borrowed from Philadelphia, where the Maugridge family lived while William worked as a shipwright and carpenter. In the outer wall of the parlor was a Bible closet for valuables. Perhaps this is where Maugridge stored documents from a Berks County judgeship he shared with Conrad Weiser.

By the middle of the 18th century, the Oley Valley was home to a dozen religious and ethnic groups. In addition to Quakers and others of English descent, there were Mennonites and Dunkards of Swiss-German heritage, Reformed Lutherans

Daniel Boone was born in 1734 in a log cabin that stood on the foundation of the left portion of this stone house. The current structure was erected by two families that owned the property after the Boones moved away.

from Sweden and Rhinelanders of French Protestant background.

In 1770 a Pennsylvania German farmer bought the Boone property. John DeTurk and his family were descendants of French Protestants who migrated to Germany. Unlike the previous owners of the house, the DeTurks followed Germanic ways. Instead of using chests of drawers, they stored their belongings in painted blanket chests. John DeTurk razed the log structure that Boone had built, replacing it with a field-stone section set on the original foundation and cellar. To cure meats, he put up a stone smoke-house. And he made the soil productive—no doubt with lime and manure.

Though they made many exterior improvements to the property, the DeTurks put little money into furnishing their house. Like other rural Pennsyl-vanians of the time, they left their floors bare, and their fireplace had no bake oven.

It is uncertain if Daniel Boone met the DeTurks when he and his wife returned to visit his boyhood area in 1781 and 1788. By then Boone had become famous for opening Kentucky to settlers. But the homestead on which he was raised provides a rare glimpse of 18th century life in a region that was neither fully frontier nor fully developed.

What to See Today

The Daniel Boone Homestead shows the lifestyles of three families during the 1700s, including Boone and his Quaker parents. Furnishings reflect the English heritage of the Boone and Maugridge families and the Germanic background of the DeTurks.

Other buildings on the premises include a well-equipped blacksmith shop and a bank barn that has a stable for farm ani-

mals and a shed with period implements. The 1737 Bertolet House, moved to the site in 1968 along with a bakehouse/smoke-house, has typical Pennsylvania German features. From the outside, the house opens into a *kuche,* or kitchen, that has a centrally located fireplace. Of later construction than the dwelling is a water-powered sawmill from around 1810, which was moved to the grounds in 1972.

As it was during Daniel Boone's childhood, the home-stead is a place of natural beauty. On the same grounds that Boone learned to know the Indians and their ways of surviving on the trail, visitors hike, picnic and fish. Recreational facilities on the site's 579 acres include overnight group camping in Wayside Lodge.

Horses graze near a late 18th century bank barn (at left) and a blacksmith shop that was moved to the homestead from a nearby town.

Landis Valley Museum

It was often hard to tell whether Henry and George Landis of Lancaster County lived in a house or a museum. From childhood until their deaths in the 1950s, they collected an enormous variety of everyday objects. Their bedrooms brimmed with old linens, musical instruments, mirrors and toys of past decades, piled almost to the ceiling. The bachelor brothers came down a stairway stashed with boxes of buttons, old lacy valentines, pow-wow books and tollgate tickets. Above their breakfast table, nearly two dozen early guns lined the wall. Above that, tankards and vases crowded a shelf. Outside, farm implements, hitching posts, anvils and two-ton millstones littered the yard.

In all, more than 200,000 relics and old objects crowded the Landis property.

The brothers were not neurotic packrats but tireless museum builders. They retired from engineering jobs early — when they were in their fifties — to devote full time to preserving items that were being replaced

by steam, electricity and gasoline engines.

From their family homestead in Landis Valley, they diligently sought objects that no one else wanted. They bought items that were gathering cobwebs in neighbor's basements and attics or were waiting for the garbage collector. They frequented auctions, taking special interest in grab-bags. Auctioneers often

threw a hodgepodge of objects into a rye-straw basket and sold the lot very cheaply. The contents of these baskets — butter prints, bookplates, mustache mugs, torn hymnals and odd assortments of bottles — became valuables. So did the baskets themselves.

Often, the brothers' engineering expertise helped them discover the purpose of items that mystified the original owner. In 1941 George paid a penny for two strange-looking objects. He astonished an antique dealer by assembling these parts to make a coffee roaster.

To many of the brothers' Pennsylvania German neighbors, the interest Henry and George took in commonplace items was odd indeed. When Henry bought

(Above) Entrance to a smokehouse — half of a reconstructed building that also houses a bake oven. (Opposite page) Aerial view of Landis Valley Museum.

an old pewter plate from a woman, she told her husband: "Henner Landis must be going off in the head. He gave me 50 cents for that plate the cats ate off of."

Thousands of similar purchases built the Landis collection. The brothers' records for 1939 show that they attended 21 auctions, made 250 private purchases and obtained 3,942 objects. During that year they spent an average of $197 a month on collecting.

When the brothers opened the Landis Valley Museum in 1925, visitors saw objects that they recognized but no longer used. "That's just like my grandmother's!" they exclaimed. Henry described the accumulated items as "reminders of the early days, how the people lived, what they did, and what they had to do it with; traditions, occupa-

Food section of the museum's reconstructed country store from the end of the 19th century.

PENNSYLVANIA'S HISTORIC PLACES

(Left) Henry Landis stands beside his brother George. On their own, with limited funds, the two men founded the Landis Valley Museum. (Below) Close-up shows chinking and a shuttered window of a reconstructed Pennsylvania German log house.

tions, and industries that have gone the way of the forgotten but have come together again at one place."

Preserving the past required quick, decisive action, Henry explained: "An old store or shop is cleared out only once; an iron kettle goes into the furnace and comes out as something else; public sales scatter heirlooms about everywhere. Therefore this is the time to salvage from general ruin these things which properly belong in a museum."

Fascinated by their roots, the brothers established their museum on a portion of land farmed by the grandson of Jacob Landis, the family's pioneer, who came to Pennsylvania from Germany in 1717. Here, just east of Neffsville, Henry and George stuffed a yellow barn with farm implements, including a wooden mould-board plow and a mid-19th century grain drill. The museum's first exhibit showed how German settlers tilled the soil, from seed to harvest, after

emigrating from the upper Rhine.

An unpretentious man, Henry never denied his rural heritage or posed as the urbane antique dealer. He and George bought to preserve, not to resell. They did so out of their own savings, parting with money in dribbles—and, no doubt, some squabbles.

(Above) Victorian detail on dormer of the Landis House, built in the 1870s. (Right) Walnut desk and bookcase (c. 1900) and a factory-made chair in the office of the Landis House. The wallpaper is original from the 1870s.

Financially constrained, they bought no Chippendale tables; in fact, they purchased very few pieces of furniture. Two striking pieces in the collection—a jelly cupboard, painted and grained, and a decorated sideboard— were wedding presents to their parents.

In addition to specific artifacts, much of the brothers' love for exploration can be traced to their father and mother. With his parents' blessing, Henry poked into his rural world as soon as he could run barefoot across the fields. Roaming along creek banks and field paths, he collected fossils, birds' nests and eggs. In addition, he reveled in learning how machines helped people to work. At the age of three, he watched workers from the Reading and Columbia Railroad install a line along the edge of the Landis family's meadow. Later, he went with his parents to visit a nickel mine, an iron furnace and a basket factory —"just to see what they were doing and how it was done," he wrote later.

When Henry won $5 for writing a winning article on "Farmers' Boys," he used the money to buy a book called *Cyclopedia of Science.* This was his first purchase for a library that eventually included thousands of books, pamphlets and old manuscripts.

Henry's boyhood fascination with the world around him soon grew into an awareness that simple rural ways were changing.

He noticed that his mother no longer hand-scrubbed the laundry over a washboard, as his grandmother did in a family photo. On the farm and in the house, factory-made goods replaced handcrafted ones. Out of this emerged a mission. He and George resolved that they would save items of the past before the objects were discarded forever.

Though the brothers collected almost anything, antique firearms became a particular interest of George's. A big game hunter in later life, George enjoyed buying and restoring weapons. While still a teenager, he discov-

The restored Landis Valley House hotel. Built in 1856, it has wide porches and hitching posts for travelers.

ered a so-called "Kentucky rifle." Crafted by Lancaster gunsmiths in the 1700s, the weapon gained wide recognition for its range and accuracy. Its name came from its popularity with frontiersmen.

Another Lancaster contribution to the march westward to the Ohio Valley was the Conestoga wagon. One of George and Henry's grandfathers had hauled flour and whiskey to Philadelphia in just such a vehicle. Three of these boat-shaped wagons found their way into the brothers' collection.

Along with large and small equipment, Henry and George collected paper art and textiles. From baskets and barrels, they unearthed many pieces that had been discarded because they did not fit modern decor. Their finds included coverlets, quilts, samplers and fine examples of fraktur, or German manuscript ink drawings. Particularly impressive are fraktur by Lancaster County schoolteacher/artist Christian Strenge and a copy by his student Christian Bachman.

The genius of the Landis brothers was not in their aesthetic sense, however, but in their eagerness to preserve the ordinary, whether it seemed beautiful or not. They hoarded everyday objects and the tools needed to make them, then made their collection available to the public. On their own, and with very little money, they created an amazing portrait of a bygone way of life.

What to See Today

The Landis Valley Museum houses the most extensive collection of Pennsylvania Ger-

(Above) The foot-pumped organ (c. 1885) in the parlor of the Landis House. (Below) Family room of the Landis House, furnished in the style of the late 1800s, when the parents of the museum's founders lived there.

man artifacts in the United States. Exhibits span a century and a half of rural life among German and Swiss immigrants to Pennsylvania, from 1750 to 1900.

The museum's 21 structures include many restored and reconstructed buildings with period furnishings. A log house and outbuildings replicate the building style of Germans who settled Lancaster County between 1760 and 1790. A brick farmstead shows the lifestyle of Mennonite blacksmith Jacob Landis and his family during the 1830s. Nearby, the 1870s Landis House is furnished as it may have been when the parents of museum founders Henry and George Landis lived there.

Other buildings include shops of a gunsmith, tinsmith, potter, blacksmith, seamstress and printer, all equipped with antique tools. These settings, as well as a tavern, hotel and country store, provide a backdrop for demonstrations of traditional trades and crafts from late spring through autumn. Buildings are open on a rotating schedule. In addition, there are historical landscapes with animals and heirloom plants. Together, the museum's scenes, structures and artifacts make it one of the finest collections of Americana in the nation.

The Landis House kitchen includes a dry sink, kerosene lamps, a 19th century canner on the Noble cookstove and ironstone table settings.

Ephrata Cloister

On a chilly spring night in the mid-18th century, the rain-swollen Cocalico Creek wound through the Ephrata Cloister, a settlement of communal mystics. Only its rush broke the stillness—until a line of singers, each carrying candles appeared at midnight. They moved, single file, each shrouded head slightly bent. From the group floated angelic music, the notes long and sweet, soaring towards the heavens. Singing antiphonally, the brothers and sisters of the community harmonized, but with little melody. In their flowing robes of white wool, the nocturnal procession entered the *Saal*, or meetinghouse, through doors so low that knees and heads had to bow.

Inside, men and women sat on opposite sides of a room that may have been one of the largest for public worship in Pennsylvania. For two hours, they listened intently to their founder and leader, German-born Conrad Beissel. With spellbinding oratory, he urged his followers to examine their lives, imploring them to be disciplined toward the

spiritual, rejecting what was frivolous and spiteful.

At times his voice rose harshly. His small, lean body tensed as he recited his beliefs, adopted from the German Baptist Brethren and other pietistic groups. Each member of the Camp of the Solitary was to seek forgiveness for any wrongdoing or bitterness before participating in these midnight watch meetings.

Beissel's views shaped the community's music, as well as its religious beliefs. For him, singing grew out of spiritual devotion. The members' heavenly tones,

rendered in a clear but small falsetto, came from hearts that were free from carnal thoughts and bodies purified by a strict diet of wheat dishes and tuberous vegetables. During four-hour practice sessions, Beissel sternly lectured the choir to focus on holy matters. The music, arranged in four, six and eight parts, seems to have resembled the tones of an Aeolian harp.

In addition to harmonies, Beissel created the words to hundreds of hymn-poems. In 1747, the community published the *Turtel Taube*, the first music book of totally American composition. Beissel composed more than two-thirds of the 300 texts in the hymnbook.

Inscribed on the music manuscripts are excellent examples of *Fraktur*, a Germanic form of illuminated writing. Women of the community painstakingly

(Above) Wood shingles and dormer windows of the Saron, *or sisters' house. (Opposite page) The* Saal, *or meetinghouse.*

Ephrata Cloister

drew the exquisite motifs with quills and ink made from gall-apple, a fungus from the oak tree.

Under Beissel's close guidance, the community developed a stylebook of calligraphy. The book includes fine scrollings and intricate floral forms that fill the inside of curving letters. Some of the finest Fraktur was created by Sister Anastasia, a beautiful and talented follower who, some people speculate, may have channeled a deep affection for Beissel into her art.

Throughout his 77 years, Beissel's charisma made him a natural leader. When he came to Pennsylvania in 1720, he did not plan to start a religious community. Instead, he sought seclusion in a cabin that he built beside Mill Creek in Lancaster County in 1723. Before long, however, people gravitated toward him.

(Above) The community added an open hearth kitchen to the meetinghouse in the 1770s, in order to prepare love feasts.

Initially these were men, but soon one of his former students, Anna Eicher, joined the group along with her sister Maria, unwittingly forming the nucleus of the future sisterhood.

When Beissel moved to Cocalico Creek in 1732 to be a hermit, people followed him again. One woman left her new husband to take up life at Ephrata. Other spouses separated, with one or both joining the Solitary, the community's celibate orders. These consisted of the Roses of Sharon for women and the Brothers of Bethania for men. Like the nearby Mennonites and Amish, members of the Solitary practiced rebaptism of believing adults and believed in pacifism.

In addition to members of the celibate orders, married couples called Householders were associated with the community. They lived on their own farms surrounding Ephrata and worshiped and worked with the other members. However, they did not participate in common ownership.

Together, the Solitary and Householders sought to practice respect for the land, mutual aid within the community and charity to people outside. Much as they desired good relations with their neighbors, however, several of the community's practices sparked heated criticism. First, group members kept the sabbath on Saturday and worked on Sunday. This offended other Christians in the area and even landed several of the brothers a brief jail sentence. In addition, neighbors disapproved of the communal lifestyle of celibate men and women and of the separation of married couples for spiritual obedience.

When his wife left home to be "rebaptized into virginity," a printer named Christopher Sauer is said to have threatened Beissel. According to an account by a member who left Ephrata, angry people twice confronted the founder in his cabin. But the community continued to flourish and attract newcomers.

One of Beissel's most famous converts was Conrad Weiser, who achieved prominence as a colonial ambassador to the Indians. He was also a political leader among the Pennsylvania

(Left) Painted standing cupboard and sleeping bench in the sisters' house. (Above) Hinged window from the sisters' residence.

Germans. For a time, Weiser was joined at the community by his wife, but she returned to Berks County to care for their young children. Later, Weiser himself left, suggesting in a letter that he was disillusioned with strife among group members.

Whatever its internal failures, the community gave generously to people around it. As new settlers poured into the Conestoga Valley, members distributed free bread. Poor children attended a German-speaking school supported by the cloister —the name later given the community as the growing town next door took the name Ephrata.

The hospitable community welcomed travelers. Visitors received a simple vegetarian meal and a straw mattress for the night—far more comfortable than the bench on which members slept, with a wooden block for a pillow.

Life at the cloister was not for the lazy. Members began the day with a song service, then spent two hours in their assigned occupation before eating breakfast. Community buildings were constructed by the members themselves, using log and half-timber design for the exterior and mixing sand, lime, pebbles and water to make mortared floor.

Work hours lengthened after Beissel placed Israel Eckerlin in charge of business affairs. Eckerlin's goal-oriented management

(Above) This original walnut door from the Saal *has wooden battens and latch and hand-wrought iron hinges. (Right) Restored well-water pump on the lawn at the cloister.*

Interior of the meetinghouse, constructed in 1741.

made the community's economy thrive. Crops prospered, as did the oil, grist, paper and fulling mills that he established. Vineyards produced wine. The tannery, bakehouse and printing press made goods demanded by Philadelphians.

Under Eckerlin, little of the profit appears to have gone to charity. Instead, the now 400 members watched capital investments grow, while Eckerlin moved to comfortable quarters and adorned himself with fancy clothes.

It was all too much for Beissel, who decided to bring spiritual order to his own house. At a love feast, he openly called for Eckerlin's dismissal. The members concurred, and destroyed all of Eckerlin's writings and records in a bonfire. They uprooted newly-planted orchards and discontinued much of their manufacturing for outside markets.

Once again, members concentrated on singing, making Fraktur and teaching at their school. Printing continued as both a business and a mission, using paper made from linen and ink from soot. Among the many books printed at the cloister were New Testaments, the community's hymnals and the book of Mennonite martyrs, *The Martyrs' Mirror.*

But the original members of the community were aging, and Beissel had lost his ability to manage the many facets of an enterprise which had grown complex. Records indicate that when Beissel had to deal with the courts during a sale of some of the community's acreage, he despaired and took to drink, as his father had in Germany. Not long before Beissel's death, he told a visitor that he was again an orphan, just as he had been following his mother's death when he was nine.

After Conrad Beissel died, Peter Miller took charge of the cloister. A capable, educated leader, he tried to steer a neutral course in the American Revolution, supporting neither the rebels nor the Tories. But the community could not turn away from people in need. When blood-stained wagons full of wounded soldiers appeared in Ephrata three days after the Battle of Brandywine, the brothers and sisters gave food and medical care to 500 of George Washington's troops.

During the winter of 1777–78, typhus, scarlet fever and "camp fever" spread through the makeshift hospital. Soldiers, sisters and Mennonite neighbors who had been helping died in the epidemic. In the aftermath, two buildings had to be destroyed because of rampant infection, and the community's storehouses stood empty.

As the 19th century dawned, only a few followers sang; even fewer worked. Religious communal life no longer attracted people. By 1813 the celibate orders had disappeared. In 1814

(Above) The print shop at Ephrata was one of the earliest in colonial America.

the remaining Householders formed the Seventh Day German Baptist Church, which used the cloister buildings until 1934.

The Vorspiel, or Prelude to a New World, of Beissel and his followers had come to an end. Yet the group's beautiful music and art remain. Scripted and printed with devotion, the songs, poems and drawings offer eloquent testimony to the faith and ability of the people who created them.

What to See Today

The extensively restored buildings of this 18th century community of Seventh Day Baptists stand along Cocalico Creek in the town of Ephrata. Medieval German in design, the log and half-timbered buildings feature dormer windows and steep gabled roofs. Architectural historian Edwin Brumbaugh — himself a descendant of community members — directed the early restoration.

A tour beginning at the Visitors Center introduces the lifestyle of the three religious orders that lived here between 1740 and 1752. Visitors can see the simple house where single women lived and the dwelling of a man living in solitude. A three-room residence for Householders, or married members, shows the more comfortable surroundings in which families stayed. Another house illustrates how the cloister's magnetic founder and leader, Conrad Beissel, lived.

The work of the community —making Fraktur, baking, spinning and weaving, candlemaking and printing—is explained by guides dressed in the white-cowled robes worn by cloister members. In the meetinghouse, where daily worship services were held, visitors can hear a recording of the distinctive, a cappella music written by community members. Not far away are the graves of Beissel and his successor, Peter Miller. Through their leadership, and the discipline and creativity of their followers, the cloister left a legacy of art and service to the needy that continues to inspire Pennsylvanians today.

(Below) Night falls on the 18th century buildings at the Ephrata Cloister.

Railroad Museum of Pennsylvania

His breath puffing into the cold night, the boy sped around a corner, feet pounding to reach the tracks before the next steam locomotive roared through town. In the distance chugged a dark, moving shadow, spewing a plume of black smoke and guided by a "golden glow" headlight. Rumbling louder, the locomotive loomed just ahead on the tracks, a massive black hulk pulling tens of thousands of pounds of freight from Altoona.

Arching on tiptoe as the train barreled past, the boy saw the silhouette of the fireman against the eerie glow of the firebox. One, two, three—17 cars, the boy counted. The driving wheels pulled the train around a curve, then eastward across a bridge. Long after the lights on the end of the caboose disappeared on the far bank of the river, the boy lingered by the tracks, lost in wonder.

To many grown-ups as well as children, a train was more than an object. To engineers who drove the rails, it seemed that the steam locomotive had a soul. The sounds the vehicle made could almost prove it. Steam hissed from the cylinders in which the pistons plunged while the blower raised the smoke. The rhythmic beat of the air-pumps sounded like breathing. When the conductor called passengers aboard, a mournful whistle sounded.

Along the tracks, the brushing sound of a moving train and the steady clicking of the wheels over the rail joints made all kinds of hopes come true. The train brought Aunt Margaret home for Christmas; sped the mail at a reliable—and sometimes amazing—pace; shipped T-rails to build more railroads; and allowed both businessmen and gamblers to pursue their endeavors enroute. "Drummers" traveled by train to introduce new goods to stores, and many a company laid its own track to connect to longer lines to ship its products. Farmers delighted in a means of transportation that could handle grain, flour, lumber and livestock.

(Near right) The John Bull, *first successful locomotive in the United States. (Opposite page) A working replica of the* John Bull *at the Railroad Museum of Pennsylvania.*

Railroads revolutionized getting from here to there. In 1800 Pennsylvanians traveled by the calendar—three weeks by wagon from Philadelphia to Pittsburgh. By 1860, people traveled by the clock—only 14 hours by train between the state's two largest cities. With high-speed diesels, the journey decreased to eight hours by 1920.

Railroads spurred people to try the seemingly impossible. In 1927 a newsreel company shot footage of Charles A. Lindbergh being honored in Washington, D.C., for his transatlantic flight. In order to get pictures to New York before its competitors did, the company developed its film on board a train. Pennsylvania Railroad's Locomotive No. 460 sped from the capital's Union Station to New York, making the 223-mile trip in a record-breaking three hours, eight minutes!

Because of their speed and comfort, and the way they expanded the economy, railroads changed the lives of Pennsylvanians more than any other industry. For more than a century, trains moved 90 percent of

the state's intercity passengers and freight. From the main railroad centers—cities such as Reading, Easton, Pittsburgh, Altoona and Harrisburg—trains threaded in all directions, whistles blowing and engines hissing.

Freight cars hauled coal, timber, minerals and fresh produce, as well as manufactured goods. Flying sparks and mechanical failures made passenger travel hazardous at first, but the beauty and comfort of coaches with velvet seats, oak paneling and brass luggage racks soon attracted people to go further than their wildest dreams of a few years earlier. In many communities, railroad depots flourished as a social hub, gathering locals as well as visitors in the way taverns did in the stagecoach era and shopping malls do today.

It was a desire to match the success of the Erie Canal in opening the West that spawned the railroads of the Keystone State. In 1834, the Main Line of

the Pennsylvania Canal was constructed to link Philadelphia and Pittsburgh. Though the line consisted mainly of waterways, it included rail connections between Philadelphia and Columbia in Lancaster County and across the mountain between Hollidaysburg and Johnstown on the Allegheny Portage Railroad.

(Upper right) This turn-of-the-century mail car enabled postal workers to sort, pick up and deliver en route. (Lower right) Elegant dining room of The Western Maryland Business Car #302.

The state government invested more than $100 million in canals, hoping that they would become a major source of revenue. Soon, however, the complex system of locks, stationary engines, gravity and horse-drawn rails became obsolete—replaced by the "iron horse" that moved forward on steam.

The first steam locomotive in the United States—the *Stourbridge Lion*—made a run from Honesdale in 1829. The first successful locomotive in the nation, the *John Bull*, was imported from England two years later. An incredible machine for its time, the 10-ton vehicle hauled loads on part of the New York-Philadelphia route for the Camden and Amboy Railroad in New Jersey—a company later absorbed by the Pennsylvania Railroad.

Pennsylvanians contributed heavily to railroad technology and practices. George Westinghouse invented the air brake and devised a uniform system to operate switches and signals. By the 1870s, his two Pittsburgh companies mass-produced these devices for railroads across the country. Civil engineer Moncure Robinson initiated the use of stone ballast to fill in railroad beds, while Philadelphia's Baldwin Locomotive Works became the world's largest locomotive builder. Founded by Matthias Baldwin, a jeweler, it manufactured 70,000 vehicles between 1832 and 1955. Baldwin himself built its first locomotive, *Old Ironsides*, in 1832.

Investors such as Stephen Girard of Philadelphia and Asa Packer of the Lehigh Valley Railroad underwrote expansion of the state's rail system. Under such presidents as J. Edgar Thompson and Alexander Cassatt of the Pennsylvania Railroad

An aerial view of the yard at the Railroad Museum of Pennsylvania shows a Reading Company turntable and radial tracks.

and Franklin B. Gowen of the Philadelphia and Reading line, rail companies gained enormous economic and political power — enough to dictate prices, squash labor protests and manipulate legislation.

The largest and most influential of these firms was the "Pennsy," or Pennsylvania Railroad. In routes and reputation, the company extended far beyond the Commonwealth — in fact, from coast to coast. One of its most famous trains, the *Broadway Limited*, carried passengers between Chicago and New York, via the state capital of Harrisburg. The company built the Horseshoe Curve to cross the

mountains west of Altoona, and earned the name "Standard Railroad" for its speed and quality of service.

Pennsylvania's rail industry reached its peak around 1915, when more than 11,000 miles of track covered the state. That figure declined steadily after World War I, as highways became a preferred means of transportation and air travel soared. But the impact of a century's dependence on trains for transportation and commerce remains — as do the memories of chugging engines, sighing brakes and the wide-eyed wonder of young and old.

What to See Today

The Railroad Museum of Pennsylvania, near Strasburg, Lancaster County, shows the development of railroads from the 1830s to the present. Artifacts range from a brakeman's lantern and builders' plates to the clock

from the tower of Philadelphia's Broad Street Station. Next door to the Visitors Center, Steinman Station re-creates the inside of a turn-of-the-century depot, complete with ornate wooden benches, a ticking wall clock and a working telegraph.

(Upper left) Steam pressure gauge on the replica of the John Bull. *(Upper right) Steam-driven whistle and steam vent on the* John Bull. *(Lower right) Trains made all sorts of dreams come true for railroad workers, children, businesspeople, families and farmers.*

The museum's main attraction is its unique collection of 65 locomotives and units of rolling stock. Vehicles include a fully-operable replica of the *John Bull*, the world's oldest locomotive. It pulls an 1855 "combine," or combination passenger and freight car, from the Cumberland Valley Railroad. Also on exhibit is a wood-burning Tahoe locomotive, built in 1875 by the industry's leading manufacturer, Baldwin Locomotive Works of Philadelphia.

Another late-19th century freight locomotive, No. 1187, is displayed in a way that allows visitors to walk underneath it, to view its structure. Several restored Pennsylvania Railroad passenger cars of the same era show the ornate furnishings for which the line was famous. In the yard, where restoration work

continues, a Reading Company turntable and radial tracks stand near the *Lindbergh Special*, which broke a speed record in 1927.

Along with exhibits, the museum houses an extensive library of historical documents and photographs. Holdings include portraits of Pennsylvania Railroad presidents and the Thomas T. Taber collection of railroad memorabilia. All are available for prearranged research.

Across the road at the Strasburg Railroad, the public can ride a train pulled by one of the museum's steam locomotives. The machine is typical of the Pennsylvania Railroad engines built at Altoona at the turn of the century, when the country ran on rails and the Keystone State was at the center of the transportation industry.

(Top) Steinman Station re-creates the inside of a turn-of-the-century depot. (Bottom) Locomotive #1187 was one of 800 Class R freight engines, the first class to be built with a Belpaire firebox.

Museum of Anthracite Mining

The early morning blast of a whistle called miners to a day without sunshine, as far as 1,000 feet down in the cold, wet earth. At 6:15, after a rapid descent down the shaft and a jolting stop at their level, Pat Caffery and his laborer, Casmir Kulesa, stepped out of the cage into the underground darkness. The flicker of their miners' lamps provided the only light.

After adjusting to the dimness, they carried their gear—a pick, shovel, drill, powder, fuses, lunchpails, ax and timber— along a gangway for almost a mile. Their rubber boots crunched in a silence darker and heavier than night, broken only by an occasional trickle of water. The lamplight from their helmets made the coal glitter. Aware of the weight just above their heads, they checked for any crumbling rock along the roof.

It was a long, eerie walk. Somewhere along the way, a doorboy opened a great wooden door that controlled the flow of air within the mine. Further on, they checked in with the fire boss, who had arrived at two in the morning to test for dangerous gases.

As they moved along the coal face they were mining, Caffery saw the safety mark chalked by the fire boss. Nevertheless, he held his safety lamp high. A blue cap on the flame meant the presence of methane, or "fire damp," a highly explosive gas. To test for "black damp"— carbon dioxide—he lowered the lamp below his knees. This gas was heavy. It would snuff out the flame of his lamp.

When the coal seams were level, Caffery and Kulesa usually mined at a right angle off the gangway. To hold the roof up, they left "pillars," or large walls of unmined coal. This was called the "pillar and breast" method.

Now, however, they pitch mined at an upward angle, deep into a seam of anthracite. It was confining work prone to roof cave-ins. Caffery crawled upward, leading the way through a narrow opening and kicking dirt onto his Polish co-worker. With gestures he showed Kulesa—a newcomer who couldn't speak English—how to timber overhead to create a manway.

After drilling and inserting dynamite into the coal, they both crept back to the main gangway. It was hard to wait but dangerous not to. Many miners were injured by returning to check a fuse.

After the charge went off, they used picks to break up the blasted coal. Caffery returned to the gangway, while Kulesa stayed in the dust-filled chamber to load the anthracite onto the mule-drawn car. Leaving first was a right claimed by the experienced, certified miners.

For veteran and newcomer alike, mining was a risky occupation. In the early days of the coal

(Opposite page) A surveyor's transit measured the angle of a coal vein and enabled a prospector to chart it on a map.

business, when safety was hardly given a nod, three miners were killed every two days in the state's anthracite region. Tens of thousands were seriously injured. Miners faced the hazards of explosions, cave-ins, gases, flooding and dust, which often caused a suffocating death from "black lung" disease years after retirement.

This dangerous but profitable industry began in the late 18th century. There are several stories of how anthracite was first discovered in the state. According to one tale, a tired hunter built a fire under what he thought was overhanging rock on Broad Mountain in Schuylkill County. The ledge, which was actually made of hard coal, began to burn.

In the early 1800s, anthracite began to gain acceptance as a clean, slow-burning fuel. In 1815, Philadelphia wire mill owners Josiah White and Erskine Hazard accidentally discovered that coal burns best with the furnace door closed and a draft passing through the fuel. In the

(Above) Necessities for an early miner included (clockwise): a water tin, pick, hat and Davidson lamp to test for methane and "black damp."

following years, U.S. manufacturers gradually turned to coal to power the nation's industrialization.

Much of the fuel came from Pennsylvania's anthracite fields, which covered 484 square miles. The hard-coal region extended from Tower City in Schuylkill County north to Forest City in Susquehanna County. With underground veins in four fields, the area remains the largest concentration of low ash anthracite in the world.

As the demand for coal grew, systems for finding it improved. After extracting cores showing the layers of the earth, surveyors drew maps of the coal seams, which often lay at sharp angles between rock strata. The formation of a particular seam guided companies in deciding whether to use drift, slope or tunnel mines to reach the coal.

Methods of getting the anthracite out, however, re-

mained largely the same. Though investors experimented with machines to extract coal, they found none that could match the strong back, nimble hands and knowledgable mind of a man. Air drills replaced hand ones, and electric and battery-operated locomotives took the place of mules to move coal cars and men. Yet most of the tools used by miners changed little over the decades.

Among the few major improvements in the mine was the development of better systems to circulate air and to remove water—up to 12 tons of liquid for every ton of coal. Two Pennsylvania companies, Worthington in Hazleton and Goyne in Ashland, manufactured a variety of pumps. These were powered by steam, compressed air or electricity.

Outside the mine, at the breaker, the 1844 Batten system of crushers and screens was the most common method of washing, crushing and grading coal. Anthracite was sold according to standardized sizes. Woe to the coal man who delivered pea-sized chunks to a household that used larger, chestnut-sized pieces in its furnace.

By wagons, rail and canal, tons of coal were shipped for use in engines, iron furnaces, and heating and cooking stoves. At the end of World War I, however, other fossil fuels began to replace anthracite. By the 1980s, the six million tons a year needed to supply the market came largely from surface strip-mining.

Over 10 billion tons of anthracite had been taken from Pennsylvania's rich fields. The coal cost a high price in health and human lives. But thanks to courageous and skilled miners, it provided heat and power, jobs and money to generations of Americans.

What to See Today

The Museum of Anthracite Mining at Ashland is one of four regional museums covering a 70-mile area in Pennsylvania's hard-coal country. Striking photos by George Harvan of Lansford show miners and the environment in which they worked. Other exhibits illustrate the variety of tools used by prospectors, engineers and miners and the development of underground safety devices. Displays include a model of the electrically powered shovel the Anthracite King and a Worthington duplex pump.

On the nearby Pioneer Tunnel Mine Tour and Lokie Ride, visitors can observe how miners once extracted coal from the Mammoth Vein.

(Left) Women hang up wash in a Pennsylvania coal town. (Above) An exhibit depicts a miner returning from underground, lunch pail in hand.

Eckley Miners' Village

"Daddy's coming!" shouted five-year-old Michael, running in from Eckley's Back Street. Mary Dziedziak made the sign of the cross, grateful that her husband had returned safely from another day in the mines. Barefoot, she stepped into the shanty behind their clapboard house and poured hot water from the coal stove for her husband's bath.

Andrew's grimy figure darkened the door. Behind him, Michael tugged for his father's lunchpail. Yanking it open, he smiled at the whole piece of bread left. He snatched it for himself, then ran to put the pail in its place in the kitchen.

Mary tested the bath water with her fingers, stained purple from berry-picking. "Ah, my woman went for huckleberries," Andrew said.

"We picked two dozen quarts," she announced. "I sold them to the company store." The 10 cents for each quart would go toward school clothes for the children.

Andrew knelt by the wooden tub and Mary washed his back — a daily ritual for a miner's wife around 1900 in the hard-coal, hardscrabble region of Pennsylvania. While he scrubbed the coal dirt from his aching limbs, Mary stirred the potatoes and cabbage in a big pot and stoked the fire to heat water for the three boarders, also Polish immigrants.

They arrived in Eckley as Andrew had — with no knowledge of English or mining and no resources except a willingness to work. With papers sent by a friend or relative working in the mines, immigrants poured into coal country to work for a pittance. Eventually, if they passed a test written in English, they

Sunset touches even a simple miner's dwelling with a golden hue.

"Breakers" cleaned and sorted coal in anthracite country. This historical re-creation was built in 1969 as a prop for the movie The Molly Maguires.

(Top) Three generations of mine workers, from Anthracite Coal Community *by Peter Roberts, 1904. (Bottom) Miners' houses in fall.*

received the pay of a full-fledged miner. When a man became a certified miner, he could apply to the company to move into a larger house.

Housing was inextricably linked to jobs, as coal companies put up "patches" or villages for mine workers. Hundreds of mining patches dotted the 10 counties where anthracite deposits are located in Pennsylvania.

In 1854, after it found coal in the area, Sharpe, Leisenring & Company put up Council Ridge colliery and built Eckley. Everyone connected with the mine lived in the patch. The mine

owners lived at the west end of town, in the largest, most elaborate houses. Foremen and superintendents lived in smaller single dwellings. First-class or contract miners—those who were certified—lived with their families in four-room houses. Unskilled laborers resided in smaller double dwellings. Many of these on Back Street had one window in each of the three small rooms. The company painted the houses red, the cheapest pigment, and trimmed the sash with black.

In a mining town, occupation and social class often corresponded to ethnic origin and

religious background. Educated and business-oriented, the mine owners were typically U.S.-born and Protestant. Welsh, English and German immigrants usually brought mining experience to the coalfields. They became foremen. Presbyterian, Lutheran or Methodist in faith, they often shared a Protestant sanctuary. In Eckley, all non-Catholic groups used either the Episcopal or the Presbyterian Church.

Many Irish reached the anthracite area between 1850 and 1870. On their heels came eastern Europeans. In Eckley, the Church of the Immaculate Conception served Roman Catholics, primarily the Irish. Except during the worst weather, eastern Europeans walked four miles to Freeland to their own ethnic churches. Each group maintained

its own language and ceremonies. In 1904, some 32 percent of the area's population was foreign-born, representing 26 different nationalities.

Social barriers were lowered during weekend baseball games and summer picnics. People from every section of town took part in these events, cheering their team or eating and buying raffle chances while the local band played. In addition to celebrations, disasters such as house fires and mine accidents sometimes brought people together. "Everybody helped," claimed one resident.

Mine owners varied in the attention they gave the town and its residents. The Coxe Brothers Coal Company, which operated the Council Ridge colliery after 1886, built the Hazleton area's

first hospital. In addition, the company established a mining and technical institute in Freeland. The company doctor, whose office stood near the homes of the mine owners on Main Street in Eckley, treated any sick resident. His income came from the dollar deducted monthly from each miner's pay.

No insurance benefited families who lost a member in the mines, but Mrs. Coxe—

(Upper left) This kitchen of an Eckley miner's family in the mid-19th century had minimal storage and a coal stove for cooking and heating. (Upper right) An outhouse stands behind one of the houses in town.

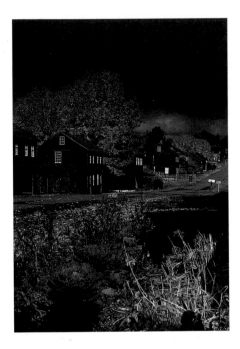

known as the "Angel of the Anthracite"—allowed widows to buy some food and clothing off the books at the company store. She paid the bill. While all residents could buy on credit at the company store, the goods there cost 15 percent more than those sold by itinerant vendors. Butchers, grocers, a repairman, a feed man and various peddlers all traveled to Eckley to sell and take orders. With the cash received every two weeks on payday, wives paid the family bills, knowing that their husbands often kept a greenback for themselves.

Mothers depended on their children, as well as their mates, for income and help with household chores. Before 1914, when a new law required children to stay in school until their 14th birthday, boys could begin working for the coal company before the age of 10. Children provided the family fuel by illegally picking coal from the

company's culm banks, or refuse piles. Youngsters rounded up the cow each day and picked beetles from the potato plants. From these plants came such staples as pierogies and potato pancakes.

Women in the coal towns had little leisure time and no place to spend it. Families had no living room; the front room served as the bedroom. Like the rest of the house, it had bare floors and whitewashed walls. The cookstove, a table and benches filled the kitchen. In summertime, when the heat became unbearable, a shanty could be used for bathing and cooking.

Household tasks were arduous. Soaking and scrubbing the soiled workclothes by hand sapped a woman's energy. When Eckley miners dreamed of the benefits electricity would bring, they often thought first of wringer washing machines for their wives.

As steam shovels and stripmining began to replace under-

(Upper left) As underground mining declined, wildflowers replaced workers. (Upper right) St. James' Episcopal Church in Eckley was organized with the help of Protestant mine operators.

ground miners in the 20th century, miners' wives took jobs outside the home. Children of mining families moved away for economic reasons. Eckley's population was 1,500 in 1870. By 1920, it had declined to less than half that number. An industry that had absorbed a potpourri of immigrants shrank. And so did company-owned communities.

What to See Today

Built by a 19th-century coal company, Eckley shows the housing and lifestyles of workers at a Luzerne County anthracite mine. On first glance, the residences may seem similar, but quality and size vary with job description. The frame house of the mine owner stands at the west end of town. Its gingerbread contrasts with the simple trim of the other dwellings. The foremen's houses are bigger than those of the first-class miners, which in turn are larger than those of the laborers. Visitors can tour representative houses, as well as the town's Protestant and Catholic churches.

The company store and coal breaker show the total dependence of residents on the mining firm. Re-creations of historic buildings, the breaker and store were erected in 1969 when Eckley served as the set for the movie *The Molly Maguires.* In the Visitors Center, exhibits portray the town's history and the day-to-day life of its residents.

Today, the underground mines that created a thriving village are quiet. But bulldozers continue to unearth surface coal above the mineshafts and tunnels of yesteryear.

(Left) Roman Catholics attended the Church of the Immaculate Conception, built in 1862. (Above) This example of a mine owner's parlor contrasts sharply with the dwellings of Eckley workers.

Pennsylvania Anthracite Heritage Museum

Timothy Carroll considered himself a refugee—far from home but lucky to be alive. Leaving famine and foreign rule in Ireland, he had set out for America on one of the over-crowded vessels that passengers called "coffin ships." Unlike thousands of other Irish in the mid-19th century, he had survived the sickness-plagued voyage. Settling with his aunt's family in St. Clair, Schuylkill County, he went to work in the mines, first underground and later in a colliery.

Carroll was a single human drop in the second wave of European immigrants to the United States. During each of two Civil War years—1863 and 1864—nearly 100,000 Irish sailed to a nation hungry for wartime workers. Like Carroll, many settled in hard-coal country in northeastern Pennsylvania.

Some of the women went to work as domestics or took factory positions, while their husbands found backbreaking jobs in mining.

The adjustment to a new life was often difficult. Many of the men's bosses were experienced miners from England and Wales who had arrived earlier. Proud of their own success in the New World, they looked with disdain on the Irish. "Papists," the English and Welsh called them, because of the newcomers' strong Catholic faith.

Resentment against these Protestant foremen and superin-tendents grew. During the time of the Molly Maguires in the 1870s, it exploded into violence. Mine bosses were murdered and Irish miners killed in retaliation.

(Left) "Breaker boys" play football in the shadow of the place where they sorted coal, exposed to dust, cold and the watchful eyes of their boss. Photo (c. 1910) from Wyoming (Pa.) Historical/Genealogical Society.

A miner attached his name tag to each coal car that he filled.

With an almost reckless determination, the Irish began to organize. They formed societies and unions, using their knowledge of English to argue for political and economic change. Quickly, they gained experience in mining and small businesses.

Soon, however, another group of immigrants joined the Irish in the coal fields. As the mining industry continued to expand, it needed more workers. Public relations efforts by coal company agents coincided with a cash crop squeeze on peasant land in Eastern Europe. Wages of $1 a day sounded princely to

(Below) A Wilkes-Barre area miner and his three children (c. 1925). Donated to Eckley Miners' Museum by Bernard Kadish. (Center above) A button crusher made finer coal. (Above right) The shoes of Evan Jenkins, a breaker boy who died at the age of nine.

these farm laborers earning 22 cents in their own countries.

So, just as Irish immigration was cresting, a wave of Poles, Ukrainians, Czechs, Slovaks, Serbs, Croats, Lithuanians, Russians and Hungarians began rippling into the anthracite area. Each nationality had its own language and culture, but English-speaking people lumped the groups together, calling them Slavs.

Wearing curious clothes and toting trunks, the newcomers threaded through the immigration system. Few could speak English. Many, like John Bosak, wore signs on their coats that indicated where they were going. Between 1880 and 1900, these immigrants grew from less than five percent of the anthracite work force to nearly 50 percent.

Less than 24 hours after arrival at one of the coal towns, these strange-speaking foreigners, usually single males, were outfitted for work. And work they did. They liked being paid by the piece, working harder to get more on payday—

more to save for their bride's passage, for a house or to have in case of emergency.

Many started out as laborers for miners. Ignorant of the system, yet trusting authority, they suffered abuse. Some miners taught their laborers only curses in English, so that the Slavs would anger the mine foremen. Sometimes lack of communication caused accidents. At the Centralia Colliery, Jacob Ruman was crushed because he misunderstood how to move a piece of heavy equipment.

Because of their economic need, Slavic families sent as many members as possible into the workplace. From the age of eight, "breaker boys" endured dust, cold and cut fingers to add $6 to $12 a month to the family income. When sons graduated to working underground—a mark of manhood—they worked their way up, eventually matching their fathers' earning of $40 to $80. As late as 1911, children contributed 35 percent of the income of the Polish families in Scranton.

Some family members earned money outside the mines. On factory assembly lines, miners' wives and daughters sewed overalls, wrapped cigars and threaded silk machines. Entrepreneurs soon realized that industries requiring workers with skilled hands could use the fuel and transport system already in place for mining. Textile mills sprouted in the coal region, especially factories that made silk. By 1910, some 20,000 women and 5,000 children worked in nearly 200 silk companies. During the peak of silk manufacturing, this region processed more than 75 percent of the raw silk used in the United States.

In addition, northeastern Pennsylvania became a major lace producing area. In 1885, the Wilkes-Barre Lace Company produced the country's first successful lace curtain. The Scranton Lace Company, a branch of a firm in England, employed close to 500 workers to make Nottingham lace.

As synthetic fibers gained popularity after World War II, the use of silk declined. Many textile mills shut down. By this time, anthracite had largely been replaced by other fuels, and most of the area's mining jobs were gone. These losses darkened the lives of residents just as coal dust had blackened their laundry. Some people moved to other regions for work, while others retreated into their own pain.

By pluck and good fortune, immigrants such as Timothy Carroll and John Bosak had survived to piece new customs and institutions into Pennsylvania's social fabric. Now, determination and luck would be needed by their American descendants as they, too, faced the challenge of building a new life.

What to See Today

Situated on a hill overlooking Scranton, the Anthracite Heritage Museum portrays the history and culture of immigrants in Pennsylvania's hard-coal region. Visitors can see heirlooms brought from various homelands, as well as artifacts related to jobs on the canals and railroads and in the factories, mills and mines.

Beside the museum is the Lackawanna Mine Tour. This underground excursion shows the setting in which coal miners worked and provides a sense of the dangers they faced.

Punch cards "program" the weave of Nottingham lace at one of the textile factories in the anthracite region.

Scranton Iron Furnaces

In 1840 in the coal town of Pottsville, Schuylkill County, a commemorative toast made the newspaper. At the Mount Carbon Hotel a group of businessmen dined to celebrate the successful smelting of iron ore with Pennsylvania anthracite.

Up to this time charcoal had been the standard fuel used in furnaces in the state, but entrepreneurs such as Nicholas Biddle believed that hard coal would produce iron at less cost. They were right. It would slice fuel costs almost in half.

Biddle saw economic growth in his glass when he raised it high that night and drank to "Old Pennsylvania — her sons, like her soil, a rough outside but solid stuff within; plenty of coal to warm her friends, plenty of iron to cool her enemies."

It was the next year that William Henry, the first American to smelt iron with the hot blast process, began building an anthracite furnace in the Lackawanna Valley northeast of Pottsville.

The wilderness area that he chose had all the essential ingredients for his smelting venture. Roaring Brook provided

(Below) Blast furnaces of the Lackawanna Iron and Coal Company. (Opposite page) Four stone towers, remnants of the Scranton furnaces, are the only 19th century stacks of their kind in the nation.

a stable power source. Surface veins of anthracite offered accessible fuel. Limestone and ore were within hauling range, and a natural bluff allowed the furnaces to be easily charged from the top.

After several false starts and alterations in design, the furnace went into blast in 1842. Henry's son-in-law Sheldon Scranton and Scranton's brother George provided financial and managerial support for the venture.

Though the furnace's location was right for making iron castings or "pigs," the site proved too remote for marketing them. So the partners turned some of the castings into finished nails, a product in great demand for building towns across the United States. Unfortunately for the investors, the nails produced by the company were so brittle that many shattered under a hammer stroke.

The company's fortune changed when it switched to manufacturing T-rail for the railroads. With funds and busi-

(Above) Arches of brick and stone are reminders of the smelting that took place in the Scranton iron furnaces, built between 1841 and 1857.

ness sense from Joseph H. Scranton, a cousin of the brothers, Lackawanna Ironworks built a rolling and puddling mill to stretch hot balls of refined iron into rail.

The effort was a huge success. Lackawanna helped to steer U.S. railroad companies away from dependence on Britain as a source of track for an expanding nation. Nicholas Biddle called the emergence of domestic rail producers a "second Declaration of Independence."

Under the Scrantons, the company grew. More furnaces were built, and the firm strengthened its reputation as an industry leader. In 1847 a sample of its rail received an award for being the finest in the nation.

Under the new name of Lackawanna Iron and Coal, the company became the third largest rail mill in the country. In 1854 steam replaced water power, and soon the company's four furnace stacks could produce more iron than any other works in the country.

To meet its voracious appetite for coal, the company developed its own anthracite mining operations. Rather than receive and ship materials by mule-drawn wagon, it laid the first rail links to the Lackawanna Valley.

In less time than it takes an infant to become an adult, the company created a thriving town. Houses and supporting industries sprouted near the plant. Immigrants with industrial experience flocked from Germany and the British Isles. Laborers from Eastern Europe found employment.

Fifteen years after the furnaces were constructed, some 7,000 people lived in Scranton, a city laid out by the company's owners. An elegant hotel, stores and a lofty Presbyterian church marked the skyline. Slag from the blast process was used to fill the swamp around present-day Courthouse Square. In 1872, Joseph Scranton built a mansion and garden on the hill overlooking the furnaces.

By the 1890s, several thousand employees depended on Lackawanna Iron and Coal's success. Scranton's population totaled 76,000—the largest of any city in northeastern Pennsylvania. From the heat and noise

near Roaring Brook rose a financial giant.

Lackawanna took pride in staying on the crest of technology. In the 1870s, the company installed two five-ton Bessemer converters and began to make steel rails. Within 20 years the company produced one-sixth of the nation's steel rail output.

Near the turn of the century, however, Andrew Carnegie's mills in Pittsburgh began to dominate the T-rail trade. Coke, which came from soft coal, replaced anthracite as the fuel of choice. To save transport costs, Lackawanna Iron and Steel moved its operations to Buffalo, New York, in 1902.

What to See Today

Four blast furnace stacks stand as remnants of one of the

busiest mills in the world. These 40-foot high, interconnected stone towers are the only 19th-century stacks of their kind in the United States.

Beneath the bridge, where workers fed the furnace and maintained heater stoves to transfer air for the blast, runs a covered passageway. Piping for the hot air blast system was located here. Behind the easternmost furnace are signs of an early anthracite mine.

Near the Scranton Iron Furnaces are reminders of the human activity generated by the mill. Hilly streets with ethnic churches and Victorian-style houses attest to Scranton's boom in the last century. The Lackawanna Station and its adjoining railroad museum illustrate the close tie of the railroads to iron production.

From this once-remote valley in Pennsylvania came iron and steel track that would cover North America in every direction. With coal and iron ore, William Henry and the Scrantons built a city. More than that, they and their workers helped to open up a vast continent.

Workers on the casting shed floor of the Lackawanna Iron and Steel Company in the 1890s. Used by permission of the Lackawanna Historical Society.

Conrad Weiser Homestead

On a hot day in June in 1744 a hopeful but uneasy group gathered in the spacious brick courthouse in Lancaster. Representatives of the colonies of Maryland and Virginia had come to the neutral ground of Pennsylvania to meet the Iroquois leaders of the Six Nations.

In the judge's chair sat the host, Governor George Thomas of Pennsylvania. On both sides of him, dressed in the wigs and ruffles of English gentlemen, sat the delegates from Maryland and Virginia.

Twenty-four Indian chiefs, shiny with bear grease and white paint, sat on the steps below. They wore furs and skins and accepted wine, punch and pipes of tobacco as tokens of welcome.

It was a meeting of two worlds —suspicious Indian and ambitious settler. Negotiations consumed two weeks, climaxing in the Treaty of Lancaster.

The success of the conference belonged to one man, colonial interpreter Conrad Weiser. His knowledge of Iroquois practices and his skill in translating Indian metaphors saved the meeting from an angry breakdown.

While a teenager, Weiser had lived with the Mohawks for a winter. He had learned Indian ways and languages and knew that little things make a difference.

Every step of the way, this Pennsylvania German helped to bridge the cultural differences between the native Americans and the colonists. He led a party of 243 Indians some 400 miles to Lancaster. En route he bought milk, flour, sheep and a steer for their nourishment, along with carefully parceled rum. He arranged for poles and boards so they could build cabins in a vacant area on the outskirts of the town, which had only been settled 16 years before.

During the negotiations, he was the consummate peace-maker. He bought tobacco by the hundredweight for the Indians and warned the high-handed colonists not to laugh at the native Americans' unfamiliar dress or behavior.

Weiser's translation showed the Indians to be far more perceptive than many colonists had thought. When the Virginia delegates said that the British king held their colony by right of conquest, the chief Gachradodon responded: "The World at the first was made on the other side of the Great Water different from what it is on this side, as may be known from the different Colour of our Skin. . . . The Great King might send you over to Conquer the Indians, but looks to Us, that God did not approve of it, if he had, he would not have Placed

(Above) German hymnbook at the home of frontier diplomat Conrad Weiser. An active churchman, Weiser wrote a number of hymns. (Opposite page) Weiser's residence and a spring-house stand in a 26-acre park in Berks County.

the Sea where it is, as the Limit between us and you."

Both the Indians and the colonists were satisfied with the Treaty of Lancaster. Besides goods, it gave the warriors of the Six Nations the right of passage to Virginia and increased their prestige with the Indians in the West. The colonists gained an ally against the French, along with the right to settle land in the Susquehanna Valley.

For 30 years, Weiser was colonial ambassador to the Indians.

Although the colonies paid him, the native Americans claimed him as one of their own. "When we adopted him, we divided him into two equal parts," the Indians said. "One we kept for ourselves and one we left for you."

Weiser kept himself planted in both worlds. A political leader in the Pennsylvania German community, he was the first President Judge of Berks County and helped to lay out Reading. He built Reading's first store and

(Above) Settlers such as the Weisers raised and processed flax to make their own clothing. (Right) Table with settings from the mid-18th century.

What to See Today

Symbolic of their kindred spirit, the grave of Conrad Weiser and the unmarked graves of several Indians stand together on his farm, now a park. On the grounds is a statue of Shikellamy, an Iroquois official whom Weiser visited.

Weiser's house is furnished with pieces from the mid-18th century. Also on display is the original deed to his property.

owned a thriving tannery. At the same time, he hosted many Indians at his farm in Womelsdorf and traveled hundreds of miles on foot to confer with Indian leaders.

One winter when war seemed imminent, Weiser set out north toward the Iroquois capital of Onandaga, to invite the Council of the Six Nations to a peace conference. Weary after six weeks' travel, and as hungry as the area's starving Indians, he collapsed in the snow. When he said he couldn't go on, his Indian companions grew silent.

Then an old man with a weather-lined face spoke: "Before, you encouraged us. Will you now give up? . . . When it goes evil with us, God has compassion on us."

Weiser got up and continued. Holding a belt of white wampum, a symbol of peace, he de-

livered his message. War preparations were halted.

Weiser's belief in peace led him to live for a time at the Ephrata Cloister. (His beard during the years with this religious community frightened the Indians.) He devoted energy to the Moravian, Reformed and Lutheran churches and despaired at their petty quarrels.

As the government distanced itself from William Penn's considerate treatment of the Indians, Weiser lost his standing as an official negotiator. Nevertheless, the Indians gave him a special tribute upon his death in 1760. At a memorial ceremony, Seneca George held a belt of white wampum streaked with black and told the colonists present, "We . . . are at a great loss . . . as well as you . . . since by his death we cannot so well understand one another."

(Upper left) Restored interior of the two-room stone house on the Conrad Weiser Homestead. The original section was built by Weiser sometime after 1729. (Upper right) The east side of the Weiser house has wooden double dutch doors.

Cornwall Iron Furnace

From the time Peter Grubb first purchased land at what is now Cornwall, Lebanon County, he dreamed of carving an empire of iron out of the wilderness. Here, in the 1730s, he bought more than 400 acres on three rounded hills. In 1742, he built a blast furnace and named it after his father's birthplace in England.

The timing and location were right for Grubb's venture. Half a dozen furnaces were already operating in Pennsylvania, but demand for iron was growing rapidly along with the colony's population. On the property Grubb had purchased, outcrops and underground rocks offered an abundance of magnetite iron ore. Dark gray with flecks of silver, these deposits were the largest that had yet been discovered in North America. In addition, rushing streams provided a source of power, and the surrounding forests offered a plentiful supply of charcoal—an important material in the smelting process.

In its early years of operation, the furnace produced pig iron

and cast-iron products for commercial purposes. During the Revolution, however, Cornwall became a major supplier of weapons for the patriot cause. On October 25, 1776, the furnace successfully cast its first cannon. Teamster John Smith hauled the 3,000-pound gun to Philadelphia for use by the U.S. Navy. Throughout the war, Cornwall made 42 cannons, 30 tons of shells and more than six tons of shot.

The furnace produced healthy profits, as well, especially after

Robert Coleman became manager. An industrious Irish immigrant, Coleman was hired by the Grubb family to be a bookkeeper. From his work, he learned the financial details of ironmaking and soon discovered that a furnace could operate on minimal cash by trading goods and services. Coleman quickly advanced, partly by marrying Ann Old, whose father owned a forge. Rising to ironmaster at a Lancaster County furnace, he invested in several iron ventures, including Cornwall. Under his management, annual production soared. Coleman himself became one of the state's first millionaires.

Coleman did not spare attention on the plant. He regularly relined and improved the furnace. In the forest, Coleman's woodcutters felled an acre of

(Upper left) Gothic Revival-style windows in the furnace building. (Opposite page) The great timber gear wheel turns on a 12-sided wooden axle.

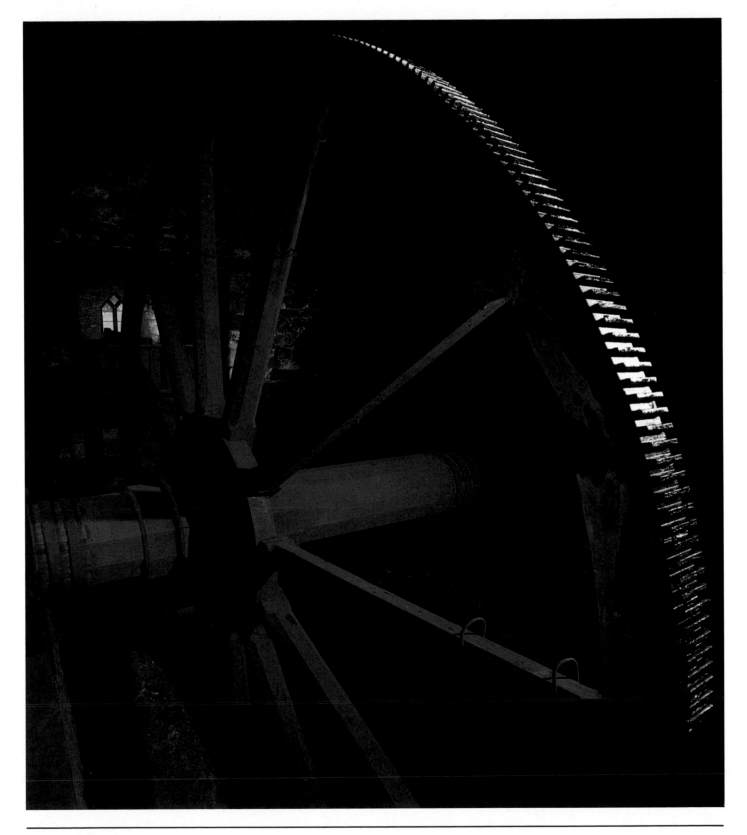

trees for each day's fuel, and colliers tended pyres of charring wood. Teamsters and their mules hauled iron ore and limestone to the furnace in wagons.

Sweaty men smudged with black dust dumped the raw materials into the hot throat of the massive furnace. From its 31-foot stack rose a fiery plume that was visible for miles away at night. The rhythmic blast of a bellows kept the glow shooting heavenward.

Cornwall was not only a factory, however, but a self-sufficient plantation, encompassing

(Upper left) A "blast book" recorded sales of iron castings and bars at Cornwall. (Upper right) The smokehouse/butcher shop was one of the subsidiary enterprises of the furnace. Cornwall was not only a factory but a self-sufficient plantation.

nearly 10,000 acres. In order to provide for the needs of metal workers on 12-hour shifts, other employees farmed, repaired roads, did smithing and constructed buildings. Workers could earn credits to buy goods from the company store or to secure other items produced on the plantation.

In 1809, Coleman left the management of his forges and furnaces to his sons and moved to Lancaster. He enjoyed renown there, but his social successes were tempered by family grief. Four of his 10 children died early —two daughters possibly by suicide.

Cornwall Furnace continued to grow for more than half a century. Its machinery was impressive. A 20-horsepower steam engine powered two wooden air cylinders, or "blowing tubs," while a huge timber gear wheel reduced the engine's speed to match that of the blowing apparatus. In 1856–57, the furnace was rebuilt. Cornwall produced

heavily up to and throughout the Civil War period, continuing to do business with many of the forges that had bought its iron bars in the 18th century.

Cornwall's final ironmaster was Robert Habersham Coleman. Like his namesake great-grandfather, Robert suffered family tragedy. His bride, Lillie Clark, died suddenly when the couple were in Europe buying furnishings for their mansion at Cornwall. Robert, who was 23 years old at the time, threw himself into his business ventures and philanthropy. He built houses and schools. He distributed Christmas turkeys to his workers, paid for their hospital expenses and provided bonuses and entertainment. On a hilltop he built Mount Gretna, a recreational community with a lake, hotel, skating rink and—to his special delight—a narrow gauge railroad.

Toward the end of the 19th century, technological advances sounded the death knell for charcoal furnaces. In 1883 Cornwall went out of blast after nearly a century and a half of ironmaking. The furnace had spanned the lifetimes of George Washington and Abraham Lincoln—of the founding and preservation of a nation. The workers and managers of the plant had been more than spectators at these events. By supplying iron for commercial and military uses, they had helped to make possible the victories at Yorktown and Appomattox and the emergence of an industrial giant.

What to See Today

Cornwall Furnace is the only fully-intact 19th century charcoal blast furnace in the United States. A prominent curator with the Smithsonian Institution called the furnace a site of "transcendent significance" and a "true survival from an important period in iron-making." Many early ironworks were made of wood and deteriorated quickly. At Cornwall, 95 percent of the

furnace is original. Massive red sandstone walls with striking Gothic Revival details show the importance of this manufacturing unit throughout its productive life.

At the Visitor Center, exhibits describe charcoal making and the iron industry. Tours proceed through a connecting shed into the furnace building, where the blast equipment and cast house are located. Particularly impressive is a mammoth timber gear wheel that turns on a 12-sided wooden axle. The tour explains the process and products of ironmaking and contrasts the lives of Cornwall workers with those of the millionaire owners.

A drive through the quiet countryside provides a view of the plantation, including the nearby ironmaster's mansion, miners' houses and an open pit iron mine. No less than the cathedral-like furnace, these bear witness to the size and energy of Cornwall—and its importance to Pennsylvania and a nation.

(Left) Charcoal wagons rest near the charging platform in the furnace building. (Above) This numbered pegboard kept a record of the "charges"— charcoal, iron ore and limestone dumped into the furnace.

Gettysburg National Military Park

For two years Union and Confederate armies had battled back and forth across Virginia. Now General Robert E. Lee was bringing the war north into the farmland of south-central Pennsylvania. His plan: to threaten Washington, Philadelphia and Baltimore by destroying the transportation networks in the area.

For several weeks Confederate bands had made raids across the "breadbasket of the North," ranging within sight of Harrisburg. Soon, after all his divisions converged, Lee's Army of Northern Virginia would mount an attack.

But the bloodiest battle of the Civil War was to begin accidentally, sparked not by a general's order but by an advertisement in a local newspaper. At dawn on July 1, 1863, a division of Confederate troops under General A.P. Hill moved east on Chambersburg Pike in search of supplies, including "fine calf boots" advertised in *The Gettysburg Compiler.* Suddenly, three miles from Gettysburg, the rebels encountered Federal cavalry scouting for General George G.

Monument to the Union soldiers of General George G. Meade's Army of the Potomac.

Meade's Army of the Potomac, which was marching north in pursuit of the Confederates.

It is hard to say which side was more chagrined at the meeting—Hill's men in gray or the mounted troops commanded by Union General John Buford. Neither party was seeking combat, but the Confederates had a large numerical advantage. Quickly, the rebels advanced toward Gettysburg, and Buford requested help from the First Corps of General John Reynolds.

Together the two officers climbed the tower of the Lutheran Theological Seminary in town to survey the attack. They concluded that the lay of the land lent itself to a defense. Reynolds, a 42-year-old from nearby Lancaster, began organiz-

ing the Union line. As he urged his men forward, the popular general was struck dead by a bullet.

Throughout July 1, General Meade ordered his army to converge on the area. When Lee learned of the encounter on the road, he consented to his troops' advance and watched as they

forced the growing divisions in blue back against Cemetery Ridge.

In the rush of fighting, relatives on opposite sides occasionally met. Corporal Rudolph Schwarz, a Union infantryman, spotted his brother among captured Confederates coming out from behind a barn. They

The Pennsylvania Memorial names almost 35,000 men from the Keystone State who fought in the Battle of Gettysburg.

had not met since leaving Germany many years before. A short while later, Rudolph was killed while his brother was led to the rear as a prisoner.

Elsewhere, an onlooker observed two virtually identical brothers—both stubby and red-haired—blubbering and hugging intermittently as they argued over which would change sides and join the other's army. The man in blue wanted his Confederate brother to join the Union ranks. The Confederate insisted that this was impossible, since the Union soldier was a prisoner.

As tens of thousands of soldiers massed around the town of 2,400 residents, casualties mounted. Lee's losses on the first day, including dead, prisoners and wounded, reached 7,000. Union casualties were higher.

Reinforcements to both sides poured in throughout the night.

Next morning, under an overcast sky with low, vapory clouds, both sides established battle positions. Behind the Union lines, surgeons scouted for sites to erect a tent hospital near a source of water. Pack mules hauled boxes of cartridges. Some men slept or fixed coffee; one soldier headed for a spring with 20 canteens slung over his shoulder. Provost Guards prodded stragglers to join their regiments. Occasionally a messenger on horseback galloped by.

Preparations consumed most of the day for the Confederates, as well. As Lee mapped out an attack, he seemed restless and irritable—perhaps due to a bout with dysentery and the oppressive heat.

Full-scale firing did not begin until 4 p.m. Shortly thereafter, Meade's line weakened when one of his fearless but rash generals, Daniel Sickles, shifted

his men to a wheat field and peach orchard, leaving Little Round Top undefended. In the nick of time, Meade's principal engineer, G.K. Warren, ordered a regiment to hold his treeless knoll "at all costs."

Union forces successfully defended this pivotal vantage point, but Sickles' troops were decimated by the Confederates of General James Longstreet. Casualties were so heavy that the wheatfield turned scarlet with blood. Sickles himself lost a leg. Propped up on a stretcher and smoking his customary cigar, he continued to give orders to his men. The general, who had entered the Army through the back door of politics, lived many years and became a strong

(Above) Monument to Battery 6, 1st New York Light Artillery. More than 160,000 Union and Confederate soldiers took part in the battle.

advocate for development of the battlefield as a military park.

Throughout the evening, regiments fought at points made famous in the annals of Civil War history—Culp's Hill, Devil's Den and Big Round Top. At the end of the second day, both sides faced a precarious situation. Lee's generals had failed to synchronize their offensives well, enabling Meade to shift his troops where needed. Yet the Union forces remained on the defensive.

Both sides had suffered horrendous losses. Lanterns of ambulances twinkled across the countryside south and west of Gettysburg, illuminating haver-

sacks, exploded caissons, mangled horses and blood-spattered bodies, some wearing gray and others blue.

That night General Meade, a tall, bearded man, called eight generals to a meeting at his headquarters. With large, dark eyes, he listened to the reports of his exhausted staff. After two hours of deliberation, the generals agreed to remain at Cemetery Ridge and to let the enemy make the next move.

Meanwhile, General Lee proposed that generals George E. Pickett and J.J. Pettigrew lead an all-out assault against the center of the Union ranks. Longstreet, Lee's second-in-command,

Union soldiers used cannons such as this one to repulse Pickett's Charge. The failure of this Confederate attack was the turning point of the battle.

objected strenuously, pointing out that the men would be easy targets as they moved uphill and across a mile of open field. Yet he agreed to organize the attack.

At 1 p.m. on July 3, General Longstreet signaled the Confederate artillery to open fire. More than 125 cannons hurled shot ranging in weight from 10 to 24 pounds. The Union artillery answered, and the resulting roar is said to have been heard as far away as Washington, D.C. Fiery projectiles splintered massive oak branches and plowed holes into the earth. The sulphur-laden air hung thick with smoke, concealing the fact that much of the rebel fire had overshot its mark.

After two hours of pounding, the guns fell silent as 12,000 Confederate men advanced toward the Union line in the largest infantry charge in U.S. history. A mass of gray more than half a mile wide marched proudly through the stifling heat, the soldiers believing that the quietness of the enemy meant that many had fallen.

As row after row of rebels came into view, the Union army gazed in disbelief. Then, muskets roared from the lines of blue. Bravely, the Confederates advanced to the stone wall marking

This memorial honors a Minnesota unit that suffered 82 per cent casualties. Gettysburg was the bloodiest battle of the Civil War.

the Union line, but they could not penetrate in hand-to-hand fighting. Eventually, what was left of the Confederate column retreated to Seminary Ridge. The rebels suffered 7,000 casualties. Lee's army was beaten.

The war itself might have ended if General Meade had counterattacked that day. President Abraham Lincoln later sharply criticized his commander for failing to push the Confederates into the rain-swollen Potomac, 50 miles to the south. The Union forces, however, had suffered heavy losses and allowed the rebels to retreat. Temporarily, Lee camped along the river. On July 13, while Meade was preparing to attack, the Confederates escaped on pontoon bridges to friendly territory.

Although the war continued for two more years, Lee was unable to launch another suc-

(Above) An equestrian statue of General George G. Meade, who commanded the Union forces at Gettysburg.

cessful offensive. Together with Grant's concurrent victory at Vicksburg, the Battle of Gettysburg tilted the conflict in favor of the Union. The cost, however, had been enormous—more than 51,000 men on both sides killed, wounded, captured or missing, in just three days of vicious fighting. Around Gettysburg, the land was ravaged. Wells were dry and crops ruined.

Four months after the battle, a local cemetery for the war dead was officially transferred to the Federal government. At a cere-

mony marking the event, President Lincoln spoke his brief and famous Gettysburg address. He paid tribute to the soldiers who had died and looked ahead to "a new birth of freedom," in a united nation without slavery. If the living dedicated themselves to this goal, he suggested, the deaths at Gettysburg would not have been in vain.

What to See Today

The 3,800-acre Gettysburg National Military Park can be toured by car, by bicycle or on foot. At the Visitor Center, an electric map provides a narrated introduction to the movements of 70,000 Confederates and 92,000 Union soldiers during the July 1–3, 1863, battle. In the Cyclorama Center, a 19th-century mural in the round illustrates Pickett's Charge—the battle's turning point and a bloody example of what happened when Napoleonic tactics met efficient firepower.

Throughout the park, a variety of markers and monuments describe the movements of specific regiments and commemorate the courage of particular individuals. The Virginia Memorial and the Pennsylvania Memorial honor the valor of Con-federate and Union troops from these states. At the Eternal Light Peace Memorial, a torch was lit on the 75th anniversary of the battle. The flame burns as a symbol of "Peace Eternal in a Nation United."

In the Gettysburg National Cemetery, visitors may walk among the gravesites and see the place where Abraham Lincoln delivered his address. Adjacent to the park stands a tribute to a military leader of the 20th century, Dwight D. Eisenhower. Visitors to the Eisenhower National Historic Site can take a self-guided tour through the home where the late President and Allied commander lived with his wife, Mamie.

A memorial commemorates the assault made by the Confederate troops of General James Longstreet.

The State Museum of Pennsylvania

It was from Asia rather than Europe that the first human inhabitants of Pennsylvania came some 12,000 years ago. During the Ice Age, Paleo Indians migrated to North America in pursuit of game. After crossing a land bridge to Alaska, these nomadic hunters moved south and east, camping in large groups, usually near a river, and hunting and gathering in small bands.

The Pennsylvania they entered was a land rich in natural resources, shaped by processes including volcanic action, shifting plates in the Earth's crust and the advance and retreat of prehistoric seas. From the remains of tiny aquatic creatures, compressed through unimaginable stetches of time, came the petroleum that would make Pennsylvania the site of the world's first oil well. From the remains of giant plants and animals, decaying under heat and pressure, came shiny, black coal.

The land was not only rich in minerals but in beauty and wildlife. In a wilderness of pine forests, grasslands and flowering plants, the Indians hunted moose, elk and deer. In addition, they stalked the seven-ton mastodon, which looked like an elephant and munched twigs and leaves.

As the Ice Age ended, the availability of food increased and the population grew. People developed a greater variety of weapons and tools in response to a more diverse natural environment. Soapstone cooking pots came into use at least 4,000 years ago. About 3,000 years ago, pottery was developed. Wet clay was coiled or laid up in slabs, then fired. With a cord-wrapped paddle, the potter welded the joints and decorated the pot.

Between approximately 500 B.C. and 1000 A.D., agriculture began to supplement hunting and fishing as a major source of food. This led to the development of permanent communities.

In the 1500s, the Susquehanna River Basin was settled by the Susquehannock Indians. The Susquehannocks depended heavily on wood as a building material and source of essential objects. To make canoes, they hollowed out green logs by repeated charring and working with stone tools. They cut bark for their roofs, carved wooden utensils and felled trees to build palisades around their settlements. If wood became scarce, entire villages of 1,000 people or more moved to another location that had sufficient trees.

Each village had a plot for agriculture. Women tended rows

(Above) Antique ice wagon of a Lancaster County dealer has chain drive and is powered by battery for day runs.

Cylindrical museum structure and its tall archives building stand to the right of state capitol in aerial view.

(Top) The Vision of William Penn, *a mural by Vincent Maragliotti, illustrates events from the state's recorded history.* (Bottom) Copper in Malachite *stone, one of the rock specimens on display at The State Museum.*

of squash, beans, tobacco and corn. After drying over a smoldering firepit, corn ears were crushed into meal with a wooden or stone muller and pestle, and stored underground.

For hunting, the men used a bow and arrow with a chipped stone tip. They fished with nets and bone hooks. Hides were stretched for use as doors, and the catch was dried and put into storage. Meats and fish may have been exchanged with other Indians for other necessities.

The native Americans viewed all living things, plant or animal, as gifts from the Great Spirit. Generosity, not charity or greed, guided their use of produce and game. They shared freely with strangers, trusting that their own needs would, in turn, be supplied by others.

The arrival of Europeans in the 16th century upset traditional Indian ways. Hunting grounds shrank, as white settlers claimed ever-increasing chunks of Indian land. The Europeans brought new diseases, against which the native Americans had no immunity, and alcoholic beverages, which made the Indians drunk. Tribes such as the Lenni Lenape, whom the whites called Delawares, became increasingly dependent upon trade with the Europeans. The Delawares' fascination with iron, brass, cloth and glass stirred antagonism between them and neighboring tribes and caused the Lenape to neglect their own crafts.

By the middle of the 18th century, most of the Delawares and Susquehannocks had died or moved west. In 1791, the Pennsylvania legislature parceled a section of land in Warren County to Seneca chief Cornplanter and his heirs. In the 1960s, however, this tract was flooded by construction of the Kinzua Dam, and the area's occupants were relocated to New York State.

For more than 10,000 years, Indians had roamed the forests, fished the streams and cultivated the fields of Pennsylvania, reverently tending the bounty bestowed over eons of natural formation and decay. In just two centuries, they lost their culture and were removed from the land. The effects of their displacement would be felt not only by their descendants, but by the land itself, as it fell into far less gentle hands.

What to See Today

Inside a circular building near the Capitol in Harrisburg, The State Museum of Pennsylvania offers a panorama of the commonwealth's human and natural history. Four floors of exhibits, both temporary and permanent, tell Pennsylvania's story from the formation of the land to the present. A sculpture of founder William Penn greets visitors, while a mural by Vincent Maragliotti entitled *The Vision of William Penn* illustrates events of the state's recorded history.

A self-guided tour invites visitors to experience Pennsylvania's past through sight, sound and touch. In the planetarium, programs show the commonwealth's place in the universe. Star positions are projected on a 30-foot dome screen. In the Hall

(Left) Life-size reconstruction of a rain forest from the Carboniferous Period. The decay of plants and animals from this period began the formation of coal in Pennsylvania. (Above) Painted pine dower chest by Christian Selser, 1775.

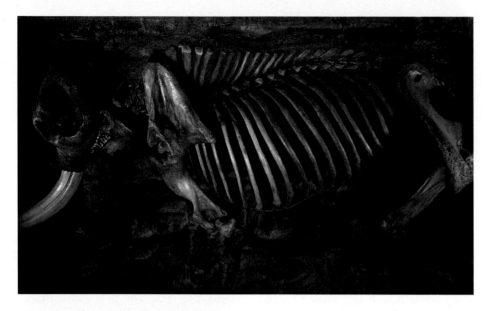

during the Pennsylvania Epoch of the Carboniferous Period — the early formative stage of Pennsylvania's coal. A separate mineral gallery exhibits excellent examples of Pennsylvania minerals.

Mammal Hall features exhibits of animals in their natural habitat, including the cougar, gray wolf and bison, which were native to the commonwealth but are now extinct here. The Hall of Natural Science and Ecology shows the plants and animals of seven ecosystems during the past 10,000 years, and explains how wildlife is threatened by acid rain, insecticides and loss of habitat.

Second-floor displays interpret the technology used by Pennsylvanians, from the tools of the native Americans to the machines and communication

of Geology, a "walk through time" interprets the formation of the state's landscape and mineral deposits, as well as the history of its plant and animal life. The high point of the walk is a realistic, life-size reconstruction of what paleontologists think a tropical rain forest looked like

(Top) Remains of a 12,000-year-old mastodon. The museum directed the removal of the skeleton from a peat bog in Monroe County in 1968. (Middle) Cast iron stoveplate by James Old of Chester County, c. 1772–73. (Right) Scene depicts the birth of a native American infant in a dome bark house.

(Left) A white-tailed deer and her twin fawns stand in a woodland habitat in the Hall of Mammals. (Above) This high-wheeler car was built by the Zimmerman family in 1909 in Auburn, Indiana, and brought to Pennsylvania by a grandson. The engine has two cylinders, horizontally opposed.

devices of the industrial era. The collections include 200 vehicles of transportation, from Conestoga wagons to a small airplane. Along with current and historical items from a variety of fields, the exhibits show how archaeology uncovers layers of the past.

Also on the second floor, the Gallery of Military History features the museum's Civil War collection—the best in the country. Exhibits include oil paintings of the Battle of Gettysburg by Peter F. Rothermel.

In the Decorative Arts and History galleries on the first floor, a variety of household and useful objects show the contributions made by craftworkers and artisans throughout Pennsylvania's history. Popular exhibits feature furniture, glassware, ceramics, clothing and kitchen utensils. A re-created village places the objects in historical perspective and provides a glimpse of what life was like in the past.

The ground floor of the musum is devoted to changing exhibits, which explore in greater depth the themes of Pennsylvania history and natural heritage.

The fine arts of the commonwealth are regularly featured, including both historical and contemporary exhibitions. A large auditorium is used for the presentation of special education programs and the performing arts.

Whether viewed in portions over a long period of time or in one comprehensive visit, the exhibits at The State Museum show the beauty of Pennsylvania's land, the variety of its people and the ingenuity behind the state's industrial and cultural development.

Pennsylvania Lumber Museum

From a hillside in Potter County, the Pennsylvania Lumber Museum faces a hump of a mountain known as Denton Hill. Now it is green with mid-age hardwoods, but locals say that it used to be bald, its timber slashed bare by the men and machines that made Pennsylvania the nation's top lumber producer in the mid-19th century and a major supplier for many years after.

Among the largest operations near the museum was Tom Fee's logging camp on Commissioner's Run. Here in the winter of 1908, "woodhicks" (as lumbermen in Pennsylvania were called) rose hours before dawn to move logs from the woods to the landings. When the air tweaked with dry cold — perfect logging weather — excitement rippled through the camp. Harnesses creaked and log chains jangled as teamsters readied the horses for a long, crisp day in the woods.

At four in the morning, the yellow circle of light from the kerosene lamps in the bunkhouse barely illuminated the empty straw mattresses of several dozen woodhicks. Wool socks still hung to dry around the

woodstove in the middle of the room, but the men were gone. They had clambered downstairs as soon as the cook beat on a dishpan to call them for breakfast.

Sitting on benches at a long, oilcloth-covered table, they bolted their food, downing it with coffee from large, enamel pots. Forks scraped across tin plates, but there was no conversation. A camp rule prohibited talking at the table.

The mood would be much different in the evening, when sweat and pipe smoke circulated in the same room. Then, woodsmen sang, played cards and

swapped stories while sitting on deacon seats made from half logs. On their days off, in town, they also drank. Lumbermen consumed enough whiskey to keep the distilleries in the area running day and night.

Preparing meals for the workers was considered the most important task in the camp. The cook, the best-paid member of the crew, rose early with his "cookees," or helpers, to make biscuits and to fry mounds of potatoes, sausage, steak, bacon and eggs. Lumbermen devoured enormous quantities of carbohydrates. A logger burned more than 8,000 calories in a day's work.

Refueled for the morning, the woodhicks donned slouch hats and made their way to the woods. The blacksmith and saw-filer stayed behind, to work in camp. The smith repaired anything made of iron. His skill in fixing hand tools and even locomotive parts, as well as

(Above) Making the first clearing for the town of Norwich, McKean County, in 1910. Photo by W. T. Clarke.

A replicated lumber camp and 1912 Shay locomotive at the Pennsylvania Lumber Museum. The locomotive pulled heavy loads of timber for short distances.

shoeing horses, made him indispensible to the camp.

Loggers were as possessive of their tools as teamsters were of their horses. A woodhick's life depended on specialized tools: a peavey that worked as a lever to move or stop logs; a pike pole to ease the pressure of a logjam on the river; and a double bit ax for notching and limbing. Lumbermen used a crosscut saw rather than an ax to fell trees. Sharpening this tool to its owner's liking endeared a saw filer to a jack. Loggers cherished a saw that could sing through a log, teeth set at an angle, pulling a continuous thread of sawdust.

Out in the woods, tasks were divided among the men. The spring before, teams hired by Tom Fee cut hemlocks on the hillside. Next, limbers and buckers took off the branches and cut the felled trees into log lengths. A scaler sized and marked each log, measuring the number of board feet it would yield. A board foot was one foot wide, one foot long and one inch thick. It was not uncommon to get 6,000 board feet from softwoods four to five feet in diameter.

In addition to the lumber it yielded, hemlock was valued for its bark. Hemlock bark was rich in tannin, a substance used in the tanning of leather. Bark peelers worked in teams of two. After the tree had been felled, one man scored the bark at four-foot intervals with an ax, while his partner removed the ringed sections with a heavy tool called a spud. The men stacked the bark in the woods until winter, when it was easier to haul.

In the early days of logging, winter was also the time to take logs out of the woods and down the mountain. Teams of horses pulled heavy sleds, piled high with logs, over skidroads that had been constructed during the summer or early fall, before the ground froze. Men called "road monkeys" covered the skidroad with water from a tank pulled by a sprinkler sled. The liquid froze overnight, and in sub-zero temperatures became very slick, ideal for moving logs across the hillside.

In the early dusk of winter afternoons, teamsters guided their horses over the skidroads by the light of flambeau torches gleaming from poles stuck in the snow. During daylight hours, other men released logs from the skid timbers holding them in

An oilcloth-covered table in the mess hall of the bunkhouse is set for loggers. In the corner is a woodbox.

(Left) The setting sun touches Denton Hill above the Pennsylvania Lumber Museum. (Below) Workers use a steam log loader near Norwich.

storage on the hill. The men rolled the logs into V-shaped slides made of round timbers and cross-skids. The heavy logs scooted down the icy chute in rapid succession, creating a noise heard for miles around as they bumped into one another. In his autobiography, Tioga County logger Philip H. Dewey wrote that a log slide was the sweetest music a lumberman ever heard, for it denoted action, and action meant success.

Men at the bottom of the mountain watched the logs accumulate in a frozen pile. From the landing, the workers could sled the logs to a local sawmill or wait until the spring thaw to float the logs downriver on a nearby stream.

What to See Today

The re-created logging camp at the Pennsylvania Lumber Museum offers a look at the industry that built the ships, houses, tools and containers of 19th century America.

Exhibits show how loggers ate, slept and worked. Old photographs illustrate how transport of wood progressed from river rafts to booms to powerful locomotives, such as the gear-driven Shay. A 1912 original is on display.

In addition, visitors can see a reconstructed steam-powered sawmill and its one-acre pond to hold logs.

As destructive as it was productive, lumbering in Pennsylvania sustained itself less than a century. An exhibit at the museum pays tribute to workers of the Civilian Conservation Corps, who replanted thousands of acres of forest over a nine-year period after the Depression.

Partially through their efforts, it is possible to drive or hike through miles of forest in Potter County—and even see deer or a bear. A likely place is near Commissioner's Run, where Tom Fee's logging camp stood.

Joseph Priestley House

Sunlight poured through northern windows into a little white-walled laboratory, illuminating tables strewn with flasks, wooden vessels and an odd assortment of glass tubes. The sun's rays gleamed on a brass microscope and sparkled through a set of Leyden jars. There was a vacuum pump and, on a standing wooden frame, a large burning glass with a compound lens. After dusk, candles would provide light for the room.

The year was 1799.

At one end of the room, a strange gurgling came from water that was being infused with carbon dioxide. The product was "soda water."

Joseph Priestley, a slender man with straight, graying hair, bent over a glass pneumatic trough. He was intent on observing the gas captured in a container over the water-filled trough. He called the substance "combined fixed air," a gas produced by heating charcoal with iron scales.

Some time ago Priestley placed a mouse in the container; it died rapidly. Now he watched the effect of the gas — carbon

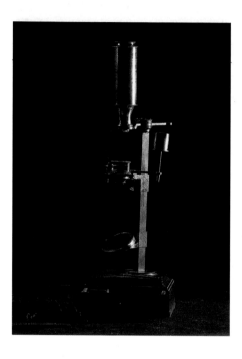

monoxide — on a mint sprig. The plant shriveled.

What a contrast to the "dephlogisticated air" that he isolated before. That substance, later to be called oxygen, made a mouse lively. The gas made blood appear red and Priestley's own "breast particularly light and easy."

An English scientist working in the hinterlands of Pennsylvania? How strange! But this corner of a new nation gathered refugees like a mother hen. Priestley needed a "happy asylum," as he

called his home in remote Northumberland. Here, far away from his persecutors in England, this scientist, theologian and educator wrote and experimented in peace.

Esteemed for discovering carbonated water and oxygen, Priestly was persona non grata in his homeland because of his unpopular religious and political views. While Anglicanism was the state religion, he was a Unitarian minister. He supported both the American and French revolutions, even dared to publish his opinions. People in England called such sympathies unpatriotic. Once, a riotous crowd destroyed his laboratory and burned his fine library.

In 1794 he came to America, no doubt drawn by his friendships with Benjamin Franklin and Dr. Benjamin Rush. After a warm welcome, he and his wife, Mary, made a difficult journey north from Philadelphia, crossing

(Above) Brass microscope used by Joseph Priestley. (Opposite page) Using equipment such as this, Priestley produced "soda water."

(Above) *The house of scientist and theologian Joseph Priestley stands facing the Susquehanna River in Northumberland.*

swollen streams and sleeping two nights in a wagon rented in Harrisburg.

The Priestleys chose four lots along the north bank of the Susquehanna River and designed a comfortable dwelling, the largest in town. But Mary died in 1796, before they could move into the house.

Northumberland's location, between two branches of the river, remained a delight to Priestley. Each fork was "as large as the Thames in London," he wrote, "bounded by rocks and hanging woods. . . ." He enjoyed the view from a balustraded deck on his steep-roofed house, his favorite spot to watch the water.

But Priestly was a doer, not a dreamer. A self-taught chemist, he was the first to show that gases have distinct qualities. During his lifetime, he identified and described nine of these

substances. Some of the hypotheses he made late in life withered because he did not accept the concept of combustion as oxidation.

In other scientific fields, Priestley left a striking legacy. He identified charcoal as an excellent conductor of electricity. One of his books, *History and Present State of Electricity*, described his friend Franklin's electrical experiments in detail.

In his *History and Present State of Discoveries relating to Vision, Light and Colours*, Priestley asserted that the retina receives visual images that are transferred to the brain by the optic nerve. In his day, this thought was as novel as his understanding of photosynthesis. "The plant restored the goodness of the air," he wrote.

But Priestley devoted more time to religion than to science. Two-thirds of his published works were theological. He believed in following Christ's teachings, but, holding to the notion that people are totally material, he rejected such mysteries as Jesus' divinity and the Trinity.

With calm demeanor, Priestley studied the questions he encountered and wrote what he found. He noted both successes and failures in his experiments. By so doing, he added considerably to the intellectual and scientific discussion of his time. Thomas Jefferson, who solicited his guidance in founding the University of Virginia, noted Priestley's contribution by calling his friend's life "one of the few lives precious to mankind."

What to See Today

The Northumberland home of Joseph Priestley features period furnishings from the late 1700s and early 1800s, when this scientist and theologian lived here with his son's family.

The classical lines of the house reveal Priestley's learned background. A central hallway lit by a fanlight window bisects the living area, which includes a library. The windows are Georgian in style; the large eight-panel ones in the parlor have solid wooden aprons made from trees with trunks 40 inches in diameter.

In the same room, a chess game is set up on a board owned by Priestley. He and Mary sometimes played three times a day.

The laboratory, located at the south end of the house, features equipment similar to that used by Priestley in his experiments. Among the pieces is a model of the large burning glass in which he identified oxygen — perhaps the most remarkable achievement of this multi-talented man.

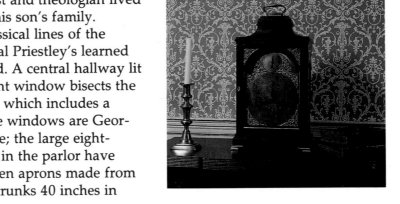

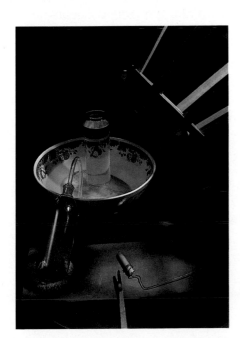

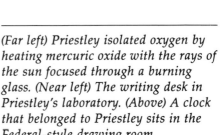

(Far left) Priestley isolated oxygen by heating mercuric oxide with the rays of the sun focused through a burning glass. (Near left) The writing desk in Priestley's laboratory. (Above) A clock that belonged to Priestley sits in the Federal-style drawing room.

Pennsylvania Military Museum

As thousands of Pennsylvanians have discovered, the reality of war has little to do with songs, the ruffle of drums or the waving of flags.

During the War of 1812, volunteers from Pennsylvania helped to repulse a British attack on Fort Erie at two o'clock in the morning. Hearing the British order to give no quarter—to kill everyone—they chose to blow up the bastion. Timber, earth, stone and bodies shot more than a hundred feet in the air. In the chaos, the enemy fled.

Sometimes officers combined daring with innovation. During the Revolutionary War, General Anthony Wayne responded to a trap by British General Cornwallis in a way that fit Wayne's nickname, Mad Anthony. When Continental troops attacked one of the British flanks, Cornwallis's main army suddenly appeared from behind its hiding place in the evergreens. Wayne ordered his men first to charge, then to retreat a few minutes later. Puzzled and wary, the British did not pursue.

On other occasions, soldiers risked their lives to save wounded comrades. In World War I in France, James Metrovitch of Pittsburgh left his company in the shelter of a stone wall and crawled 30 yards under fire to his wounded commander. Putting the officer on his back, he carried him to safety. Both men survived, and Metrovitch received the Congressional Medal of Honor.

Not every outcome was so happy. During World War II, the plane on which Archibald Mathies was a gunner was hit by enemy fire, killing one co-pilot and knocking the other unconscious. Rather than leave the injured pilot and parachute to safety, Mathies volunteered to try to land the aircraft. He died in a crash landing. In Vietnam, William D. Port of Petersburg ran into the line of fire to help a wounded member of his company. Then he hurled himself in front of a grenade, dying as he shielded three comrades from the explosion. Mathies and Port were awarded the Medal of Honor posthumously.

Heroism of another sort was shown by soldiers who endured long waits under terrible conditions. In the trenches of World War I, Pennsylvanians of the 28th Division hunched in the

(Left) Pouch and uniform of a member of the 28th Division, A.E.F., in 1918.

Soldiers send messages at a command post in the museum's re-creation of a World War I battlefield.

They immediately gathered under an oak tree in front of the Donegal Presbyterian Church to receive their marching orders.

The love of homeland that motivated these soldiers would certainly have been understood by the commonwealth's founder, William Penn. Yet Penn would have deeply regretted the involvement of Pennsylvanians in military efforts. As a Quaker, Penn did not believe in war of any kind, and he envisioned his colony as a peaceable kingdom in which disputes would be settled nonviolently. Because of this, he ignored the title of Captain-General that was assigned to him in his charter, and he declined to fortify his towns as neighboring colonies had.

Penn's position was supported by the Pennsylvania Assembly, in which Quakers held a majority. However, as the population of non-pacifist groups in

mud for days, in wet, dirty clothes. The men crawled over one another, in order to stay out of enemy fire. Rats and lice were frequent visitors.

Over the years, many Pennsylvanians have volunteered for the armed forces. In 1777, Scotch-Irish farmers in Lancaster County heard during a church service that the British were planning to occupy Philadelphia.

(Above) An 1890 model of the Vickers-Maxim machine gun. (Right) The 28th Division, in which many Pennsylvanians served, parades along Arch Street in Philadelphia after the end of World War I.

Pennsylvania increased and the French began to threaten the colony's borders, the Assembly changed its stand against military expenditures. Noting that the legislators had allocated money for beef, pork, flour, wheat and "other grain," Benjamin Franklin suggested that the colony buy grains of gunpowder. The Assembly members agreed.

Nevertheless, the legislature continued to withhold funds needed to build stockades on the frontier. People there were irate. With Conrad Weiser as their spokesman, angry Germans stormed the State House and demanded defense legislation. Quakers split on the issue. With the support of some, led by Isaac Norris, the Assembly passed the Militia Act of 1755. The military force created by the Act is a direct ancestor of the Pennsylvania National Guard.

In the years since, a few Pennsylvanians have held to the pacifist principles of William Penn. Many others have fought for commonwealth and country in a wide variety of conflicts. The merits of the two positions are still in debate. The courage of the soldiers who suffered and died, however, is not.

What to See Today

The Pennsylvania Military Museum in Boalsburg traces the commonwealth's participation in wars from the time of the colonial militia to the Vietnam draft. Indoor displays include a Hall of Weapons, a photo gallery with scenes of military training, recruiting posters, and memorabilia from several wars.

A special exhibit re-creates a World War I battlefield. Walking through a trench activates sounds of machine-gun fire and dialogue between soldiers. On display outside are mortars and a German artillery piece from that war.

The 71 acres on which the museum is located memorialize the 28th Division, composed largely of Pennsylvanians, which fought in World War I. The land was donated by Colonel Theodore D. Boal, who formed Company A, the first U.S. cavalry machine-gun troop. Colonel Boal trained the members of the company on this soil before their assignment to the 28th.

Plaques on a Memorial Wall list 28th Division officers killed in action. Across a stone-arch bridge over Spring Creek stand other monuments dedicated to World War I veterans. One of these memorials, a tribute to the 28th Division's 107th Field Artillery, invites visitors to "gaze on the beautiful mountains and valleys of Pennsylvania. All this beauty is yours to enjoy because men have fought and died to preserve it. God grant that this country will always enjoy freedom of speech, freedom of religion, freedom from want and freedom from fear."

(Above) Replica of a battle-damaged house in France during the first World War.

Somerset Historical Center

Adam Miller was familiar with hardships. Striking out across the Allegheny Mountains at the end of the 18th century, he staked a claim in isolated western Pennsylvania.

There, he and other settlers survived by their own pluck. Few roads crossed the wooded wild, so each family had to be self-sufficient. Food was sparse. In the winter, howling winds blew cold drafts between the logs of cramped cabins.

Iron tools and utensils were rare. Furniture and kitchen equipment had to be painstakingly crafted. To make clothes, settlers raised sheep and grew flax, then processed the fibers into yarn and thread. The resulting fibers were spun and woven into linen or woolen cloth, then sewn into garments. A combination of linen and wool produced a warm, durable fabric called linsey woolsey.

When stockings wore out, people stuffed leaves into their shoes. Families gathered straw and chaff for their beds and chopped wood for the fire. There was little time for baths and none for laundry.

Only a few hardy souls persevered through such adversity. Yet Miller, a stouthearted farmer of German background, called his homestead "Paradise."

He and other settlers thrust themselves into pioneering with their eyes open. Dreams of owning land and giving their children a better life drove people westward. Some came from Virginia, others from the towns of the East and directly from Europe. Newcomers plodded along Forbes Road and Braddock's Trail, built during the French and Indian War in the 1750s and '60s.

Typically, a farmer and his wife walked beside a horse or two and sometimes a cow, each animal packed with tools and other necessities. Missionary David McClure wrote of seeing a baby strapped securely on top of

(Above) Maple sap flows through a wooden spile into a "keeler," or collection bucket. (Opposite page) A walking spinning wheel, with flax and naturally dyed wool overhead and uncombed wool in a basket at right.

The cramped house of settler Adam Miller includes a rope bed, cradle, fireplace, table with foods and apple peeler, and cupboard.

a family's belongings. The husband carried his gun and an ax, McClure said, while the man's wife had the rim of a spinning wheel in one hand and a loaf of bread in the other. Efficient movers, they had wound their bed rope around the cow's horns.

Through similar ingenuity, pioneers survived crises on the frontier. When one man spied his chicken eating melon seeds that were lying out to dry for next year's planting, he cut open the fowl's crop to regain the seeds. Then he sewed up the chicken so the family would continue to have eggs.

Certainly, Adam Miller needed equal inventiveness as he carved out a life in Somerset County. Here, near the highest mountain in the state, the land was beautiful but dangerous, rich but untamed. Glades of high bluegrass sporadically interrupted acres of virgin timber. Streams meandered through the plateau, and tree trunks were so wide that two men could not reach around them.

Winters were harsh, but the forests in the area offered a natural crop in springtime — maple sugar. On warm days following freezing nights, the sap in the maple trees ran. To collect it, settlers bored a hole into the trunk of a tree and inserted a wooden spile to direct the flow. A "keeler," or bucket, that was hung on the spile caught the sap, a clear liquid that looked like water.

To keep the sap from spoiling, boiling had to begin immediately. Night and day, a family tended the wood fire. The evaporation process was slow; 50 gallons of sap yielded only one gallon of syrup. Most families boiled the liquid even further, until it crystallized into maple sugar. This could be stored and preserved more easily than syrup.

(Left) A cooper made barrels and keelers for collecting maple sap. This exhibit displays the tools and products of coopering. (Above) Flax spinning wheel and clock reel (c. 1800).

As the population of the area grew, sugaring became a social event. At the end of a good season, a family invited its neighbors to a "sugarin' off" party. Jokes and games made the long hours of stirring evaporate along with the syrup. Party-goers shared in eating the Pennsylvania German treat called Spotza— hot, thickened syrup poured over snow.

With a sense of community came economic growth and an easier way of life. By and by, farmers such as Adam Miller replaced their original cabins with two-story dwellings of hewn logs, chinked with wood or stone and daubed clay for snugness. They built more outbuildings and acquired household items, glass for windows and farm implements.

By the time the children of the settlers were adults, local orchards produced apples, and livestock and gardens offered a wide variety of foods. Soon machine-made goods and real coffee would be available in a general store.

What to See Today

Built in 1800, Adam Miller's restored home stands on a grassy

Winter scene at the Somerset Historical Center.

knoll at the Somerset Historical Center, 10 miles from the cottage's original location. Furnishings in the two-story structure show how he and other settlers provided for food and clothing. Artifacts and demonstrations explain basket-making, maple sugaring and the making of textiles from flax and wool. Nearby are fields of corn, flax and wheat, and a garden filled with vegetables and herbs.

Also on the grounds are a rare smokehouse from the early 19th century and a replicated log barn. An exhibit of farm implements shows tools similar to those Miller used, including a wooden plow with a straight moldboard. There are a grain cradle and drop reaper, as well as an 1850 decorated grain thresher. An 1885 corn husker and shredder, which removed the husks and cut up the fodder, would have astounded the original settlers.

A walk past Miller's house and across an 1859 covered bridge leads to a restored maple sugar camp in the woods. Elsewhere, a typical 1900 kitchen and general store portray the conveniences that would have been used by Miller's great-grandchildren. Together, all of these displays show the change in lifestyle over four generations, as improved roads, rail lines and steam power opened up the state's rural southwest.

(Above left) The restored house of Adam Miller stands on a grassy knoll 10 miles from its original location. (Above right) Artifacts and demonstrations explain the making of textiles from flax and wool.

Bushy Run Battlefield

In the 18th century, Europe's disputes made North America a battleground and turned native Americans into pawns of two invading nations. Each taking Indian allies, Britain and France fought for nine years in a conflict called the French and Indian War.

For the tribes of the colonial West, the British victory in 1763 seemed to produce only broken promises. Why did British troops remain in western Pennsylvania after the end of the war? the Indians wondered. An English proclamation in 1761—made to pacify the Indians—forbade further settlement west of the Alleghenies. So why were homesteads, even taverns, popping up in the area?

The Indians saw their own communities dwindling. One settlement near Pittsburgh was nearly wiped out by smallpox after its residents received infected blankets. The British traded less and gave fewer gifts than the French. How would the Indians survive?

Pontiac, an Ottawa chief, inspired his people to rise in rebellion against Fort Detroit. Other tribes, including the Shawnees and Delawares, followed with attacks on other British forts and civilian settlements.

Sunset at the place of Colonel Henry Bouquet's victory over the Indians, which marked a turning point in Pontiac's Rebellion on the frontier.

(Above) Oil painting of Colonel Henry Bouquet, who led British troops in the Battle of Bushy Run, August 4–5, 1763.

After a series of Indian victories, the British devised a plan to safeguard the frontier. They assigned Colonel Henry Bouquet, a Swiss mercenary, to reopen connections with beseiged Fort Pitt and bring the defenders much-needed supplies.

Bouquet set out from Carlisle on July 18 with approximately 450 well-trained men — mostly Pennsylvanians — and wagons of supplies. The journey west was draining. The men sloshed through creeks, climbed mountains and cut roads. Their wool uniforms must have scratched in the summer heat.

Along the way, the soldiers passed empty fields and houses abandoned by settlers out of fear. In three columns, each 40 yards apart, the troops marched on with dread.

The army rested two days at Fort Ligonier. There the men transferred their flour from barrels to bags, shifting them onto packhorses. Without wagons and with their muskets half-cocked, they moved rapidly toward Bushy Run, a planned rest stop.

About noon on August 5, when the sweaty, tired troops were only a mile from their destination, shots rang from the woods. Members of the advance guard fell. From behind the trees the Indians fired, then returned to cover.

Immediately, the British found trees and formed a defensive circle. Both sides shot as fast as they could load. Gunsmoke added to the haze of the humid day. The wounded were carried to the rear on litters of flour bags.

The firing continued until dark, musket balls flying from all sides. When the shooting stopped, Bouquet assembled his troops in a clearing on a nearby knoll. Here they built a circular fortification out of bags of flour.

Inside the enclosure, the wounded lay begging for water. According to legend, several men stole into the woods to a spring and carried water back in their hats.

All spent an anxious night. In his diary, Bouquet bemoaned the horrors of fighting in a wilderness that offered "no refreshment for the healthy, nor relief for the sick." Towns and hospitals were far away in the settled East. Surrounding the clearing were trees with trunks wide enough for two Indians to hide behind each.

At dawn, the native Americans resumed shooting. Stealthily, they fired, disappeared and reappeared. In contrast to the British, they wore little except breechclouts and moccasins. Their bodies were painted black, and their earlobes were slit and wrapped in brass wire that stretched down to their shoulders.

Each Indian wore a scalplock — a circle of hair in the middle of the head. The rest of the hair was plucked. Some tufts were greased and stood out straight.

With the British troops weary and suffering heavy casualties, Bouquet changed tactics. He ordered the front of the line to

Ligionier blue rock—a local limestone—the memorial stands where a fortification of flour bags guarded the British soldiers on August 6, 1763, the second day of their battle against the Indians.

Nearby rises a tall oak, the only living thing that may have been alive at the time of Colonel Henry Bouquet's victory.

In addition to touring and hiking the 183-acre site, visitors can see displays of clothes and weapons used by the Indian warriors and British infantrymen who fought at Bushy Run.

fake a retreat over the top of Edge Hill, in order to draw the native Americans out of their cover.

The ploy worked. The Indians rushed into the opening and met muskets and bayonets of troops who had formed a circle. The remaining British companies hit the Indians with full fire.

Unable to hold their position, the native Americans fled, with Bouquet's men in pursuit. The British chased the Indians for two miles, then marched 12 miles on to rescue Fort Pitt.

Bouquet's victory broke the uprising, later called Pontiac's Rebellion. A defeated people, the Delawares and Shawnees moved west toward the Ohio Valley in an attempt to restore their shattered way of life.

What to See Today

A stone memorial marks Edge Hill, one of two grassy knolls at Bushy Run Battlefield. Made of

(Above) A monument of Ligonier Blue Rock marks the spot of Bouquet's defense during the last day of the Battle of Bushy Run.

Fort Pitt Museum

They called it "the Point" — that vital triangle of land that jutted out between two rivers, the Monongahela and the Allegheny. Both France and Britain wanted it and fought to possess and fortify it. The furor that this finger of turf ignited in the 18th century fired the French and Indian War. Whoever controlled the Point — the cradle of a city that would later be called Pittsburgh — faced the Ohio River flowing westward and dreamed of owning all the land beyond it.

In the 1750s, the French placed control of the Point among their highest priorities in North America. They claimed land from the Gulf of St. Lawrence in Canada through the Great Lakes region, and south to Louisiana. Between Quebec in the north and New Orleans, near the Gulf of Mexico, lay 3,000 roadless miles. The French needed the 987-mile-long Ohio to supply their scattered trading posts and prevent incursions by competing nations.

In April of 1754, a force of 500 French and Indians arrived at the forks in 60 flat-bottomed boats and 300 canoes. Before they began to build Fort Duquesne, they evicted a small garrison of English who had been sent to trade on behalf of the Ohio Company. The hasty departure of the English with their tools and guns spelled the end of the gloriously named Fort Prince George.

From Fort Pitt, built on "the Point" in 1764, the city of Pittsburgh grew along the banks of the area's three rivers.

Later encounters between the two nations were less genteel. In his first and most controversial battle, 21-year-old Colonel George Washington attacked a French encampment 50 miles south of the Point. The camp's commander, Coulon de Jumonville, was killed. His brother, Captain Coulon de Villiers, set out from Fort Duquesne with 650 troops, in search of revenge. In a driving rain, he attacked Washington and his men at Fort Necessity, a ramshackle stockade. After two wretched days, with corpses lying in bloody pools and the injured crowded and hungry, the two sides signed a truce. A dejected Washington returned east to Virginia.

The following year, Washington came back to the area—this time with British General Edward Braddock and his well equipped army. The battle at Fort Necessity had drawn Britain and France into the French and Indian War, and Fort Duquesne was a major prize. With his red-coated Irish and colonists in buckskin, Braddock carved a road across the Allegheny Mountains and marched toward the Point.

Terrified of the devastation British cannons would wreak on the fort, French Captain Pierre de Contrecoeur decided to take

(Above) Model of Fort Pitt shows its location where the Monongahela and Allegheny rivers join.

the offensive. In a brilliant strategic move, he surprised the British in a narrow ravine six miles from the fort. More than a third of Braddock's 1,500 men were killed, along with the general himself. The 250 French and 600 Indian allies suffered only 16 casualties. They returned to Fort Duquesne, gloating over their spoil—500 horses and 100 oxen.

Over the next few months, the French and their native American allies launched a series of attacks on Pennsylvania

settlements, using Fort Duquesne as a base. Finally, in 1758, Britain's General John Forbes set out from Carlisle to capture the Point. His men cut a 100-mile route wide enough for wagons over steep mountain grades. Sick and weak, Forbes left the day-to-day work to Colonel Henry Bouquet. Bouquet trained the British forces to defend themselves against the ambush tactics of the Indians. Along the way, the soldiers built and fortified small posts.

Cautiously, the British advanced on Fort Duquesne, expecting the French to fight with every resource. Instead, they found what Forbes called "total desolation and wreckage." The French had destroyed the fort rather than defend it.

Forbes envisioned a British phoenix rising from the French ashes. In a letter datelined "Pittsbourgh," he wrote Prime Minister William Pitt in London that he was renaming the fort after him. Soon, Forbes predicted, the newly-gained territory along the Ohio would be "the richest and most fertile of any possessed by the British in North America."

It seemed impossible that the French would simply concede such an area, so the British worked to strengthen the fort against attack. They built temporary palisades in 1759, but remained uneasy. Although

French power was virtually in shreds, the British built a 17½-acre fortress — the strongest they ever erected in America. Some 66,000 cubic yards of dirt were removed in digging the foundations. The earth was used to construct ramparts and other defenses, as well as casemates and magazines sunk at least five feet underground. Beyond the fort's perimeter, five redoubts enabled soldiers to fire from two levels while safeguarded from sniper fire.

Meanwhile, outside the fort, a town took shape. Settlers built a sawmill, limestone kilns, forges and shops for coopering and smithing. Vast fields of Indian corn, oats and rye stretched out from the barracks.

The official end to the French and Indian War in 1763, along

with Bouquet's defeat of the Indians the following year in Pontiac's Rebellion, lessened the need for Fort Pitt. With no threat in the vicinity, the British allowed it to deteriorate. In 1792, U.S. forces abandoned it.

Coveted and contested for its military importance, the Point took on peacetime significance as the center of a growing city on the frontier of an expanding nation.

What to See Today

The Fort Pitt Museum in Point State Park tells the history of the French and Indian War in western Pennsylvania. The 80 displays include a replica of a trading post, artifacts excavated along the route of Britain's General Braddock, the interior of a barrack in the fort and 18th century armaments. In addition, visitors can view fort construction techniques and a model of Fort Pitt.

Nothing remains of the largest British post in North America. Only a redoubt, known as "the Blockhouse," stands. It is open for public visitation during scheduled hours.

(Left) Replica of a trading post, a setting that brought Indians and British into contact. (Top) Pennsylvania rifle used on the frontier in the 1700s.

Flagship Niagara

On an August day in 1813, a fleet of U.S. warships set out from a Pennsylvania port for a fateful battle. The encounter between the U.S. forces of Commodore Oliver Hazard Perry and the British fleet of Captain Robert Barclay proved to be one of the most decisive engagements in U.S. naval history. Yet it did not take place on the open sea but in the middle of Lake Erie, in the heart of the North American wilderness.

Barely 30 years after the war of independence ended, the United States was again fighting the country from which it had sprung. Though the U.S. war slogan was "Free Trade and Sailors' Rights," the conflict stemmed largely from a desire for land. Pioneers craved the woods along the Great Lakes, an area inhabited by Indians under British domination.

In the Congressional elections of 1810, a group of fiery young nationalists came to office. They argued that the British supported Indian confederation, and thus

deserved to be routed once for all. In addition, a series of incidents on the Atlantic, involving British ships and U.S. sailors, led to cries for revenge.

In 1812, Congress declared war. The British quickly captured Detroit and other U.S. coastal settlements in the Northwest Territory. To regain control of the area, President Madison ordered a fleet to be built on the shore of Lake Erie.

The construction of warships on Presque Isle Bay must have been an odd sight. Here, in a natural harbor protected from storms and the watchful British, Commodore Perry and Daniel Dobbins supervised construction of the *Lawrence* and the *Niagara,* along with four smaller vessels.

The town of Erie had only 500 residents, so carpenters, blacksmiths and shipjoiners had to be brought in from Philadelphia, New York and New England. Lumber was in abundant local supply, but other building materials had to be transported from hundreds of miles away. Tools were hard to obtain; the first workers even had to make their own axes.

In July of 1813, the arduous construction was completed. But

(Above) Knotted deck rope on the United States Brig Niagara.

Detail photograph of the Niagara *taken from the painting* **The Battle of Lake Erie** *by Julian O. Davidson, 1885/1887. Photo by D. James Dee. Courtesy of Lynn S. Beman, Beman Galleries, Nyack, New York.*

before Perry could confront the British, he faced a final logistical challenge. The two brigs, weighing 260 tons each, had to be hauled across a shallow sandbar to reach the lake beyond the bay.

Fortunately, on July 31, the British ships that had been blockading the bay sailed away toward Canada. At dawn the next day, Perry's men began to maneuver the ships across the bar, using wooden devices called "camels," or scows. Day and night, the men labored. When they realized they had to strip the ships in order to reduce their weight, they worked frantically, fearing the British might reappear at any moment.

By August 4, the two brigs cleared the bar. Perry's men then rearmed the vessels.

With his ships fully manned, Perry took command of the *Lawrence* and assigned recently promoted Jesse Elliott to command the *Niagara*. The U.S. squadron of 10 small warships, six built in Erie and four converted merchantmen, sailed to western Lake Erie to support the army of Major General William Henry Harrison and to blockade the British at Fort Malden, Ontario.

As the sun rose on September 10 at Put-in-Bay near Sandusky, Ohio, the British fleet appeared, led by Captain Barclay's flagship, the *Detroit*. The two squadrons were of comparable strength, but the British ships had longer-range guns. When the fleets were a mile apart, the British opened fire.

At that distance, only two guns on the *Lawrence* could reach the enemy. Perry closed range as fast as possible, because the heavy cannons of the U.S. ships would be superior at close range to those of the enemy.

(Above) Commodore Oliver Hazard Perry, *portrait by Gilbert Stuart and Jane Stuart. Courtesy of the Toledo Museum of Art, Toledo, Ohio. (Right) Detail of the U.S. Brig* Niagara, *from which Commodore Perry led the U.S. fleet to victory in the Battle of Lake Erie.*

Perry's flagship received heavy bombardment. Smoke obscured the clear morning, and shattered bodies covered the deck.

The ship's doctor was so busy he could only stop bleeding and amputate limbs hanging on by a shred of flesh. His assistants, meanwhile, came from the wardroom below to take the place of dead gunners.

British shot had shredded the sails and rigging of the *Lawrence*, making the ship impossible to maneuver. By 2:30 p.m. the brig was defenseless, with 80 percent of the crew killed or wounded.

For reasons that remain puzzling, the *Niagara* had hung back during the hours that the *Lawrence* fought valiantly. Now, instead of surrendering, Perry boarded a rowboat to carry on the battle from the undamaged brig.

Aboard the *Niagara*, he signaled for close action and penetrated the British line within 15 minutes. Soon after 3 p.m., all the cannons were still, and Captain Barclay surrendered his entire squadron.

That afternoon Perry informed General Harrison of his victory. His proud but brief letter stated: "We have met the enemy and they are ours, Two ships, two brigs, one schooner and one sloop."

The victory enabled the U.S. army to push north, ending the British threat to the Northwest Territory.

What to See Today

Restored in 1988 and 1989, the U.S. Brig *Niagara* is one of three surviving Navy warships from the early 19th century. The square-rigged, two-masted vessel is docked along the waterfront in the city of Erie, near the site of its original construction.

Aside from the use of specially treated lumber, the brig was rebuilt using the same techniques originally used by Commodore Perry's workers. Some pieces of the original hull have been incorporated in the new hull. Below decks are cramped quarters for the officers and men, as well as a sail bin, fireplace, storerooms and magazines. In 1813, the 155 crew members slept on hammocks on this deck.

The cannons on the *Niagara* are replicas of those used in the victory over the British. There are two 12-pound long guns and 18 short-range carronades that fire 32-pound shot.

In addition to showing a superb piece of maritime restoration, tours of the *Niagara* bring to life an important chapter in the War of 1812.

(Above) Restored wooden bow of the Niagara, *one of three surviving Navy warships from the early 19th century.*

Drake Well Museum

August 1859. Summer in Venango County was sizzling toward its finish. All night the frogs croaked along Oil Creek near Titusville. By day a steam engine whirred in a nearby clearing.

The sound of a drill bit pounding into solid bedrock brought out only a few doubting residents. Most of the locals had lost interest in the venture of that crazy man from New England. Wearing a black suit and top hat, "Colonel" Edwin L. Drake had been prospecting for oil for 15 months. People were surprised that this likable, even-natured gentleman continued in such a wild venture.

Though oil was not unknown to the local residents, the idea that large amounts of it could be extracted by drilling struck them as highly unrealistic. But Drake believed that there was plenty of this greasy black substance underground. William A. Smith,

his blacksmith and driller, had often seen it bubble up with natural gas in springs or appear at salt wells. Lighter than water, it had floated on the eddies of the creek for years, annoying the frogs. Years before, the Seneca Indians in the area had smeared the thick ooze on their bodies for decoration and medicine.

A former train conductor, Drake had been hired by James

M. Townsend of the Seneca Oil Company to find oil in quantity. The investment had been spurred by scientific research which suggested that petroleum had remarkable lighting and lubricating qualities. In Pittsburgh, for example, Samuel Kier had been refining oil for several years with a distilling apparatus. Whale oil was becoming expensive. Kier believed that petroleum

Derricks poked skyward in oil boom-towns, after Drake showed petroleum could be extracted by drilling.

(Above left) Drake's original well at Titusville, Pennsylvania. (Above right) The Sanderson cyclone drilling rig was the first portable oil rig.

could replace it as a home lighting source.

Inside the wooden engine shed, Smith steadied the drill as it ground into the earth. Powered by steam, it was going down at the rate of three feet a day. How far would they have to drill? Years of sinking salt wells had taught Smith, known as "Uncle Billy," to be prepared. He had about 300 yards of rope on hand.

Delays had dogged the project, but the Colonel and Uncle Billy persisted. When lining the shaft with wood did not keep out the groundwater, they drove an iron pipe down to bedrock. The first one broke, so Drake ordered a stronger one and Smith welded its lengths together. With no engine lathe nearby, the driller had to use his best smithing skills to make the drilling tools.

Uncle Billy listened closely as the drill cut through sandstone inside the iron casing. At 69 feet, the sound changed, and the rope moved more quickly. The drill had dropped into a six-inch crevice. Since it was late Saturday, the drilling tools were pulled up for rest until Monday.

But the next afternoon, Uncle Billy strolled over to the engine house from his home to inspect the progress. Squinting his eye over the pipe, he noticed a dark liquid about 10 feet down. Could this be true? Excited, he pulled up a sample in a makeshift tin container. He recognized the dirty, greenish grease immediately. Oil!

The news spread quickly. On Monday people teemed about the site to see the most significant event in Titusville. Drake responded calmly. Now that he had struck oil, he needed to find containers to hold it. The Smith family's washtubs were already full; with much difficulty, Drake acquired whiskey barrels. Although the well was not a gusher—and everyone was too excited to gauge its flow—it would produce about 20 barrels a day. A new industry was born.

Excitement in Titusville touched off a six-year oil boom in the surrounding countryside. People believed that they could get rich faster than the gold-seekers had in California a decade earlier. Prospectors "kicked down a well" using a primitive spring pole and foot power. Frenzied investors pooled money and speculators rushed to farmers to lease land for drilling. All along Oil Creek and the Allegheny River, wooden derricks poked skyward, and shacks took the place of trees in muddy, oil-stained boomtowns.

One of the most fleeting, Pithole, lasted less than a year and a half. In January 1865, I.N. Frazier and James Faulkner leased land on the Holmden farm, far from the other wells. Pithole started when they hit a gusher—250 barrels a day. A settlement of three log cabins swelled to a town of more than 15,000 people and 57 hotels! The end of the Civil War contributed to the stampede, as did the nearby drilling of more fast-flowing wells.

Five hundred lots were laid out along 22 streets. By summer the wells near Pithole Creek were pumping 2,000 barrels a day, and wooden structures sprang out of the mud and rubble. There was not one brick or stone building in town.

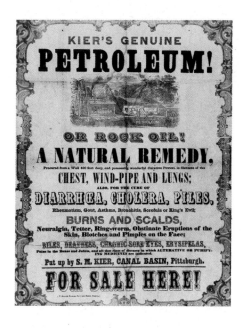

(Left) The 1865 Densmore car transported large twin drums of oil by rail. (Above) Pittsburgh advertisement promotes the virtues of petroleum.

Like other oil communities, Pithole was a firetrap. The gas near wells ignited easily and consumed wooden buildings like kindling. Water tanks on wheels were useless to extinguish the black smoke fires that raged across creeks and from one storage tank to another.

Despite numerous blazes, Pithole's population soared. The post office became the third busiest in the state, after Philadelphia and Pittsburgh. The town had no running water, so huge amounts of liquor slid across the bars. Crowds at Murphy's Theater topped a thousand. Concerts, balls and church events brought residents inside, off the oozing mud of the streets.

From this ramshackle town, the world's first successful oil pipeline was laid by Samuel Van Syckel. The line, which ran to a railhead along Oil Creek, revolutionized the transport of bulk liquids. Teamsters, coopers and bargemen protested, but they could not compete with a system that reduced shipping costs by two thirds.

As the number of derricks in Pithole rose, the oil flow of all of them diminished. Nobody, including Drake, realized that the oil came from the same source. By the end of 1866, lessees tore down their wooden structures. More people lost money than gained.

Neither Drake nor Uncle Billy grew wealthy. A few months after the landmark drilling, Drake's derrick burned. He put up a second, but the well went dry. In 1873, the Pennsylvania General Assembly voted Drake an annual pension of $1500. He died in Bethlehem, in the eastern part of the state, in 1880.

(Above) Steam engine powers the drill at the replica of Drake's well. (Right) Fires occurred frequently in oil towns.

PENNSYLVANIA'S HISTORIC PLACES

lighting. The museum library contains the largest collection anywhere of materials on the origins and development of the oil industry. In addition, it houses fine photographs of the Pennsylvania oil boom.

Several displays focus on the Venango County story: the investors; the discoverers, Colonel Drake and Uncle Billy Smith; the boomtowns; and photographer John Mather, who graphically recorded the boom. Despite the wane of the Pennsylvania oil industry after 1866, the state still keeps a toehold in the industry. According to one display, the paraffin base of Pennsylvania petroleum makes it the best lubricating oil in the world.

Though his financial reward was modest, he had given a start to a huge industry and opened the way for a world beyond his imagining.

What to See Today

Scenic Oil Creek winds along the lush grounds of Drake Well Museum in the northwestern part of the state. Along its banks stand artifacts that illuminate the history of oil production. These include a metal standard rig, the Densmore car for rail transport, a spring pole like those used by prospectors, and mystery pits dug thousands of years ago to collect oil, perhaps by the mound-builders. On the actual site where Edwin L. Drake drilled the first oil well stands a replica of his derrick and engine house.

The more than 70 exhibits in the museum explain how oil is formed, the technology of oil production and storage, and the processes by which petroleum is refined for lubrication and

(Above) The Colonel Drake fire engine, built in 1868 to fight oil fires.

Old Economy Village

The scene must have astonished travelers on the Pennsylvania frontier in 1838. In the midst of a wilderness where most people lived in one-room log houses, rose a thriving German village. On Sunday, hundreds of men and women poured from their neat two-story brick houses in answer to the church bell. On wide, tree-lined streets, they walked briskly to worship.

Inside the church, men and women took seats on opposite sides of the center aisle. Together they sang a hymn, their voices ringing clear as the mystical, ethereal words rose toward heaven. Standing still with their hands clasped together on their breasts, they listened to a fervent prayer, the words as Lutheran as their heritage.

These immigrants were members of the Harmonist Society, a religious community that focused on readiness for Christ's return. Here at Economy, north of Pittsburgh, they believed that they had progressed to an ad-

vanced state of holiness—a reason for joy.

With rapt attention, they listened as their founder delivered a sermon on Christian hope. A tall, white-haired man in his seventies, George Rapp spoke in a vigorous voice that belied his age. His blue eyes sparkled under shaggy brows, as he compared the Society to one of the faithful congregations in the New Testament book of Revelation. Rapp encouraged each

member to follow God's calling and to accept God's will with complete abandonment. He interpreted this practically, urging husbands, for example, to withhold criticism even if their wives served potatoes three times a day.

Living in harmony with oneself, with others and with God prepared Society members for Christ's return and thousand-year reign on earth, Rapp continued. With a plea to Christ to come—"Behold, thy children are ready"—Rapp dismissed his followers to eat and relax in their homes, the private side of this American Utopia.

For nearby settlers, who endured harsh living conditions,

(Above) Window of Harmonist store in Economy. (Opposite page) Flower beds line the walk to the house of Frederick Rapp, Economy's business manager.

(Above) The George Rapp house faces Church Street in present-day Ambridge. Rapp and his followers founded Economy in 1824 on 3,000 acres near the Ohio River.

the village of Economy must have seemed like heaven on earth. The Harmonists, or Rappists, lived peacefully in comfortable houses. They ate satisfying meals five times a day and mixed meaningful work with worship—all with no worry for their personal welfare. In accordance with the New Testament book of Acts, everyone worked for, and benefited from, the Society. There was no individual ownership.

Along with financial sharing, the Society members believed in celibacy as a way to purify themselves for Christ's return. Single members were expected not to marry and married members to refrain from conjugal intercourse.

The Harmonist Society began in the late 18th century, when Rapp, a 30-year-old weaver in

Württemberg, Germany, began meeting in homes with a group of Separatists. Rapp and the others believed that the official, Lutheran, church had failed to practice the teachings of Christ. In 1803, after German authorities refused permission for the new group to establish a religious community, Rapp set out to find land in Pennsylvania. His adopted son, Frederick, stayed behind to organize transportation to the New World for 300 families.

To finance the new settlement, all of the members sold their belongings and pooled the proceeds. "This is very rich land," Rapp assured his followers in a letter. "Everything grows in sufficient abundance. . . . Whoever wants to work here can obtain enough wealth." Moreover, "There is religious freedom. . . . ," he continued. People "want you to think and believe what you wish, only be an honest man, that is esteemed."

Originally, Rapp's followers established a community on land he had purchased in present-day Butler County. The group relocated along the Wabash River in southern Indiana in 1814, only to return to Pennsylvania 10 years later to build Economy on 3,000 acres southwest of the first settlement.

The most successful of the Harmonist settlements, Economy confirmed Rapp's glowing assessment of the opportunities available in America. At Economy, everyone in the community practiced a trade or skill under the supervision of a foreman. Women worked eight hours a day, men 10 hours, at such tasks as milling flour, herding cattle,

tending the fields and making leather goods, soap and shoes.

Over time, Economy developed an impressive range of industries. Members raised flocks of Merino and Saxon sheep for fine woolens. Silkworms from hundreds of mulberry trees turned out award-winning silk. Vines were grown along the walls of buildings, so that the warm bricks could sweeten the grapes for wines of European quality. Community members distilled whiskey. Eventually, nine factories produced goods from cutlery to gingham to pottery for the outside world.

Home life in Economy was organized around households of up to eight people, men and women under the same roof. Each of these "families" kept three gardens—for herbs, vegetables and flowers. Two

(Left) Reception room in the George Rapp house is furnished with an 1860s wool ingrain carpet, a Harmonist clock, an 1820s Lustreware tea set and a religious painting by Dutch artist Frans Floris. (Above) Dining room of the Romelius Baker house.

adjacent households shared an outhouse, a root cellar and a shed, in which a cow and chickens were kept. In each home, a woman designated as housekeeper prepared meals and cleaned.

The miller and butcher delivered flour and fresh meat daily. Clothing, foodstuffs and other items were available on request from the community store. These goods were free to members, although the store kept track of transactions for inventory purposes. Outsiders often made purchases at the community store and sold items to the Society. They also used the village post office.

Like the Ephrata Cloister a century earlier, Economy was a place of music and art, as well as thriving commerce. Each member owned a psalter, and as early as 1825 the Society owned an Albrecht piano. On Sunday afternoons, members met in the music room to learn songs, both sacred and whimsical. Singing with an instrumental ensemble was a special feature of celebra-

(Above) Working reproduction of one of the water pumps that stood on every block at Economy. Underground pipes carried water through town. (Right) Piano, flowers and a copy of Benjamin West's Christ Healing the Sick *(c. 1815) show the Harmonists' appreciation for art and music.*

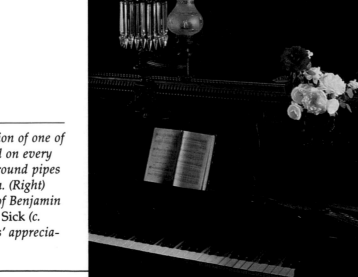

tions held in the Feast Hall, which was notable for its gambrel roof. On the second floor, in a room 100 feet long and 50 feet wide, more than 600 Harmonists celebrated the Lord's Supper and love feasts. The hall rang with voices, accompanied by strings and brass.

Society members valued cultural experiences that would increase their worthiness for Christ's coming. They kept informed of the operas opening in Philadelphia and bought paintings by European masters. Members created artwork to celebrate God's handiwork, rather than to showcase individual talent. In 1826, a Natural History and Fine Arts Museum opened on the main floor of the Feast Hall. The museum displayed stuffed animals, including an elk, an eagle and an alligator, as well as an antique chest in which, according to tradition, William Penn stored his treaty with the Delaware Indians.

Education received more emphasis at Economy than in most frontier settlements. The Harmonists operated their own school for children of members and some orphans adopted from the outside. Every resident could read and write, and adult education classes met in the evening.

For contemplation, members often retreated to the formal garden — a reminder of the Garden of Eden. Two blocks away, near an array of blooming flowers, stood a statue of a woman holding a lyre. The way to the statue, called "Harmony," was blocked by a complex maze. This arrangement reminded the Rappists that reaching a state of unity and serenity was not easy.

George Rapp himself learned this lesson when he lost to a deceiver in 1831. Anticipating Christ's future kingdom on earth, the Harmonist leader fell easy prey to an outsider who claimed he could pave the way for the millenium. Impressed by the man's seal and gold-inked signature, Rapp admitted him into the community. After an extended stay, the visitor lured many of the Society's youngest and strongest members away from Economy. Among these was the Society's doctor, Christoph Mueller. A man of varied talents, Mueller also served as printer and schoolmaster.

Despite these setbacks, the community continued to prosper. In anticipation of the Second Coming, the community stashed half a million dollars in gold and silver in a stone vault. After Frederick Rapp's death in 1834 and George's in 1847, at the age of 90, investments in oil and railroads replaced manufacturing. As always, the group kept a year's supply of grain in a granary built with half timber and stone nogging.

By the start of the 20th century, however, Economy's few remaining members were aged and investments were neglected. Production had virtually stopped. In 1905, the Society was dissolved. During

(Above) Flatbed printing press in the Mechanics Building, the only such press in the United States that is displayed in its historical setting.

the next decade, the Commonwealth of Pennsylvania acquired a portion of the town.

Some of the objects from Economy were sold after the Society's closing, but the one-handed clock on the church steeple still remained. Crafted by Harmonists, the clock had been installed by Rapp so that his followers would not watch the minutes, but only the hours as they prepared for Christ's return. The community members continued in expectation of this event as long as they lived. One by one, they were buried in graves without name markers, in order to preserve the communal

equality that had characterized life at Economy over three quarters of a century.

What to See Today

Old Economy Village in Beaver County shows how life was lived in George Rapp's Harmonist Society between 1824 and 1830. Visitors can see 17 restored structures with more than 16,000 objects used by members of this religious community.

Laid out in the style of a German village, Economy features well-kept gardens and walkways. Bright beds of antique flower varieties — snapdragons, pansies, lilies, campanella, German strawflowers, lunaria and fiery splendens—line paths that radiate from a lily pond.

In the artisans' shops, many of the tools used in the 19th century remain. The cabinet-maker's shop features three-foot lathes, a pedal-operating mortising tool and planes for making mouldings. The print shop has a wooden, flatbed printing press, the only one in the United States that is displayed in its historical setting.

In the Romelius Baker house, the choice and arrangement of furniture show the Harmonists' European origins. Outside are a working pump and kitchen garden. Furnishings in the homes of George and Frederick Rapp illustrate the appreciation the Society's leaders had for fine and decorative arts.

The lushness of the town's greenery and the refined peacefulness of its dwellings point to the Harmonist ideals of serenity and joy. The members of this utopian society sought to keep their inner lives as pristine and productive as Economy, the picturesque German village.

(Below) Cloak room of the Romelius Baker house, one of 17 restored structures at Economy.

Addresses

Brandywine Battlefield
P.O. Box 202
Chadds Ford, PA 19317
(215) 459-3342
U.S. 1, Delaware County

Bushy Run Battlefield
Bushy Run Road
Jeannette, PA 15644
(412) 527-5584
Pa. 993 northwest of Greensburg, Westmoreland County

Conrad Weiser Homestead
R.D. #1, Box 28
Womelsdorf, PA 19567
(215) 589-2934
U.S. 422 at Womelsdorf, Berks County

Cornwall Iron Furnace
Rexmont Road at Boyd Street
P.O. Box 251
Cornwall, PA 17016
(717) 272-9711
Off Pa. 419 in Lebanon County

Daniel Boone Homestead
R.D. #2, Box 162
Birdsboro, PA 19508
(215) 582-4900
One mile north of U.S. 422, near Baumstown, Berks County

Drake Well Museum
R.D. #3
Titusville, PA 16354
(814) 827-2797
Off Pa. 8 near Titusville,
Venango County

Eckley Miners' Village
Rural Route 2, Box 236
Weatherly, PA 18255
(717) 636-2070 or 2071
Eight miles east of Hazleton off Pa. 940,
Luzerne County

Ephrata Cloister
632 West Main Street
Ephrata, PA 17522
(717) 733-6600
Near junction, U.S. 322 and Pa. 272,
Ephrata, Lancaster County

Flagship Niagara
80 State Street
Erie, PA 16507
(814) 454-1973
West Front Street, Erie

Fort Pitt Museum
101 Commonwealth Place
Point State Park
Pittsburgh, PA 15222
(412) 281-9285
Downtown Pittsburgh

Graeme Park
859 County Line Road
Horsham, PA 19044
(215) 343-0965 or 2223
West of Pa. 611 on County Line Road
near Horsham, Montgomery County

Gettysburg National Military Park
Gettysburg, PA 17325
(717) 334-1124
Off U.S. 15 at Gettysburg

Hope Lodge
553 Bethlehem Pike
Fort Washington, PA 19034
(215) 646-1595
Pa. Turnpike exit 26 south near Fort
Washington on Old Bethlehem Pike,
Montgomery County

**Hopewell Furnace National
Historic Site**
R.D. 1, Box 345
Elverson, PA 19520
(215) 582-8773
Pa. Turnpike exit 22 to Pa. 345 south of
Birdsboro, Berks County

Independence National Historical Park
313 Walnut Street
Philadelphia, PA 19106
(215) 597-7086 or 7120
Visitor Center at 3rd and Chestnut

Joseph Priestley House
472 Priestly Avenue
Northumberland, PA 17857
(717) 473-9474
Priestley Avenue near U.S. 11 and Pa.
147 intersection, Northumberland,
Northumberland County

Landis Valley Museum
2451 Kissel Hill Road
Lancaster, PA 17601
(717) 569-0401
Pa. 272 north of Lancaster

Morton Homestead
Write: 1900 Pattison Avenue
Philadelphia, PA 19145
(215) 583-7221
Pa. 420, Prospect Park,
Delaware County

Museum of Anthracite Mining
17th and Pine Streets
Ashland, PA 17921
(717) 875-4708
From I-81 exit 36-W via Pa. 61 to
17th and Pine Streets, Ashland,
Schuylkill County

Old Economy Village
14th and Church Streets
Ambridge, PA 15003
(412) 266-4500
Pa. 65, Ambridge, Beaver County

Pennsbury Manor
400 Pennsbury Memorial Lane
Morrisville, PA 19067
(215) 946-0400
Near U.S. 1 and 13 south of Morrisville,
Bucks County

**Pennsylvania Anthracite Heritage
Museum**
R.D. 1, Bald Mountain Road
(McDade Park)
Scranton, PA 18504
(717) 963-4804 or 4845
I-81 exit 57-B or Pa. Turnpike exit
38 to McDade Park, off Keyser
Avenue, Scranton

Pennsylvania Lumber Museum
P.O. Box K
Galeton, PA 16922
(814) 435-2652
U.S. 6 at Denton Hill State Park,
Potter County

Pennsylvania Military Museum
P.O. Box 148
Boalsburg, PA 16827
(814) 466-6263
U.S. 322, Boalsburg, Centre County

Pottsgrove Manor
West King Street
Pottstown, PA 19464
(215) 326-4014
Pottstown, Montgomery County

Railroad Museum of Pennsylvania
Box 15
Strasburg, PA 17579
(717) 687-8628
Across Pa. 741 from railroad station,
Strasburg, Lancaster County

Scranton Iron Furnaces
Located on Cedar Avenue
Write: R.D. 1, Bald Mountain Road
Scranton, PA 18504
(717) 963-3208
Cedar Avenue, downtown Scranton

Somerset Historical Center
R.D. 2, Box 238
Somerset, PA 15501
(814) 445-6077
Pa. Turnpike exit 10 north on Pa. 985
from Somerset, Somerset County

The State Museum of Pennsylvania
P.O. Box 1026
Harrisburg, PA 17108-1026
(717) 787-4978
Third and North Streets, Harrisburg

Valley Forge National Historical Park
P.O. Box 953
Valley Forge, PA 19481
(215) 783-7700
Pa. Turnpike exit 24 north on U.S. 422

Washington Crossing Historic Park
P.O. Box 103
Washington Crossing, PA 18977
(215) 493-4076
Pa. 32 and 532, Bucks County

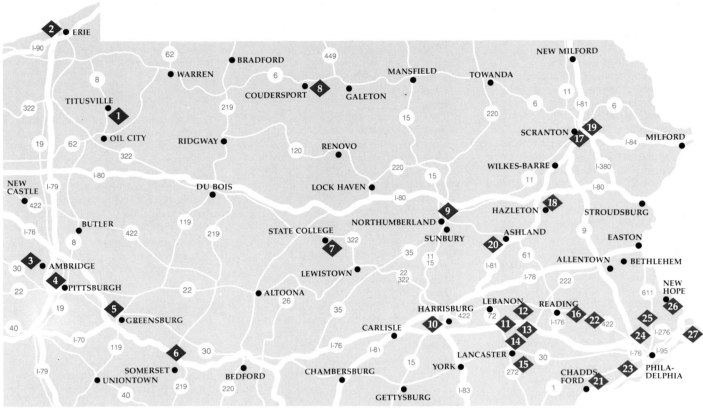

1 DRAKE WELL MUSEUM

2 FLAGSHIP NIAGARA

3 OLD ECONOMY VILLAGE

4 FORT PITT MUSEUM

5 BUSHY RUN BATTLEFIELD

6 SOMERSET HISTORICAL CENTER

7 PENNSYLVANIA MILITARY MUSEUM

8 PENNSYLVANIA LUMBER MUSEUM

9 JOSEPH PRIESTLEY HOUSE

10 THE STATE MUSEUM OF PENNSYLVANIA/THE PENNSYLVANIA STATE ARCHIVES

11 CORNWALL IRON FURNACE

12 CONRAD WEISER HOMESTEAD

13 EPHRATA CLOISTER

14 LANDIS VALLEY MUSEUM

15 RAILROAD MUSEUM OF PENNSYLVANIA

16 DANIEL BOONE HOMESTEAD

17 THE PENNSYLVANIA ANTHRACITE HERITAGE MUSEUM

18 ECKLEY MINERS' VILLAGE

19 SCRANTON IRON FURNACES

20 MUSEUM OF ANTHRACITE MINING

21 BRANDYWINE BATTLEFIELD

22 POTTSGROVE MANOR

23 MORTON HOMESTEAD

24 HOPE LODGE/MATHER MILL

25 GRAEME PARK

26 WASHINGTON CROSSING HISTORIC PARK

27 PENNSBURY MANOR

Readings and Sources

Brandywine Battlefield

Gifford, Edward S. *The American Revolution in the Delaware Valley.* Philadelphia: Pennsylvania Society of Sons of the Revolution, 1976.

Jackson, John W. *With the British Army in Philadelphia, 1777–1778.* San Rafael, Calif.: Presidio Press, 1979.

Smith, Samuel Stelle. *The Battle of Brandywine.* Monmouth Beach, N.J.: Philip Freneau Press, 1976.

Bushy Run Battlefield

Anderson, Niles. *The Battle of Bushy Run.* Harrisburg: Pennsylvania Historical and Museum Commission, 1966. 19 pp.

O'Meara, Walter. *Guns at the Forks.* Englewood Cliffs, N.J.: Prentice-Hall, 1965.

Peckham, Howard H. *Pontiac and the Indian Uprising.* Princeton: Princeton University Press, 1947.

Conrad Weiser Homestead

Richter, Daniel K., and James H. Merrell, eds. *Beyond the Covenant Chain: The Iroquois and Their Neighbors in Indian North America, 1600–1800.* Syracuse: Syracuse University Press, 1987.

Wallace, Paul A. W. *Conrad Weiser: Friend of Colonist and Mohawk.* Philadelphia: University of Pennsylvania Press, 1945.

Wallace, Paul A. W. *Indians in Pennsylvania,* revised edition. Harrisburg: Pennsylvania Historical and Museum Commission, 1972.

Cornwall Iron Furnace

Bining, Arthur C. *Pennsylvania Iron Manufacture in the Eighteenth Century.* Harrisburg: Pennsylvania Historical and Museum Commission, 1973.

Noble, Richard E. *The Touch of Time: Robert Habersham Coleman, 1856–1930.* Lebanon, Pa.: Lebanon County Historical Society, 1983.

Walker, Joseph E. "Negro Labor in the Charcoal Iron Industry of Southeastern Pennsylvania," *Pennsylvania Magazine of History and Biography.* 93 (Oct. 1969): 466–486.

Daniel Boone Homestead

Elliott, Lawrence. *The Long Hunter: A New Life of Daniel Boone.* New York: Reader's Digest Press, 1975.

Lofaro, Michael A. *The Life and Adventures of Daniel Boone.* Lexington: University Press of Kentucky, 1986.

Wallace, Paul A. W. *Daniel Boone in Pennsylvania.* Harrisburg: Pennsylvania Historical and Museum Commission, 1987. 20 pp.

Drake Well

Dolson, Hildegarde. *The Great Oildorado: The Gaudy and Turbulent Years of the First Oil Rush, Pennsylvania, 1859–1860.* New York: Random House, 1959.

Giddens, Paul H. *The Birth of the Oil Industry.* New York: Macmillan, 1938.

Miller, Ernest C. *Pennsylvania's Oil Industry.* University Park: Pennsylvania Historical Association, 1974. 69 pp.

Eckley Miners' Village

Broehl, Wayne G., Jr. *The Molly Maguires.* Cambridge: Harvard University Press, 1964.

Miller, Donald L., and Richard E. Sharpless. *The Kingdom of Coal: Work, Enterprise and Ethnic Communities in the Mine Fields.* Philadelphia: University of Pennsylvania Press, 1985.

Wallace, Anthony F. C. *St. Clair: A Nineteenth-Century Coal Town's Experience with a Disaster-Prone Industry.* New York: Alfred A. Knopf, 1987.

Ephrata Cloister

Alderfer, E. Gordon. *The Ephrata Commune: An Early American Counterculture.* Pittsburgh: University of Pittsburgh Press, 1985.

Doll, Eugene E. *The Ephrata Cloister: An Introduction.* Ephrata: Ephrata Cloister Associates, 1958. 32 pp.

Reichmann, Felix, and Eugene E. Doll. *Ephrata As Seen by Contemporaries.* Allentown: Pennsylvania German Folklore Society, 1952.

Flagship Niagara

Dillon, Richard. *We Have Met the Enemy: Oliver Hazard Perry, Wilderness Commodore.* New York: McGraw-Hill, 1978.

Rosenberg, Max. *The Building of Perry's Fleet on Lake Erie, 1812–1813.* Harrisburg: Pennsylvania Historical and Museum Commission, 1974. 72 pp.

Sapio, Victor. *Pennsylvania and the War of 1812.* Lexington: University Press of Kentucky, 1970.

Fort Pitt Museum

Bird, Harrison. *Battle for a Continent: The French and Indian War, 1754–1763.* New York: Oxford University Press, 1965.

Downes, Randolph C. *Council Fires on the Upper Ohio: A Narrative of Indian Affairs in the Upper Ohio Valley until 1795.* Pittsburgh: University of Pittsburgh Press, 1968.

Stotz, Charles Morse. *Outposts of the War for Empire: The French and English in Western Pennsylvania, Their Arms, Their Forts, Their People, 1749–1764.* Pittsburgh: Historical Society of Western Pennsylvania, 1985.

Gettysburg National Military Park

Luvaas, Jay, and Harold W. Nelson. *The U.S. Army War College Guide to the Battle of Gettysburg.* Carlisle, Pa.: South Mountain Press, 1986.

Nye, Wilbur S. *Here Come the Rebels!* Baton Rouge: Louisiana State University Press, 1965.

Tucker, Glenn. *High Tide at Gettysburg: The Campaign in Pennsylvania.* Morningside Bookshop, 1973.

Graeme Park

Gentile, Nancy Jacquelyn. *The Penrose Family at Graeme Park.* Harrisburg: Pennsylvania Historical and Museum Commission, 1984. 62 pp.

Loeper, John J. *Elizabeth Graeme Ferguson of Graeme Park.* Hatboro, Pa.: Hatborough Historical Society, 1974. 25 pp.

Tully, Alan. *William Penn's Legacy: Politics and Social Structure in Provincial Pennsylvania, 1726–1755.* Baltimore: Johns Hopkins University Press, 1977.

Hope Lodge

Andrews, Wayne. *Architecture, Ambition, and Americans: A Social History of American Architecture.* New York: Free Press, 1978.

Tolles, Frederick B. *Meeting House and Counting House: The Quaker Merchants of Colonial Philadelphia, 1682–1763.* New York: W. W. Norton, 1963.

Wallace, Paul A. W. "Historic Hope Lodge," *Pennsylvania Magazine of History and Biography,* 86 (April 1962): 115–142.

Hopewell Furnace National Historic Site

Lewis, W. David, and Walter Hugins. *Hopewell Furnace: A Guide to Hopewell Village National Historic Site.* Washington: National Park Service, 1983.

Paskoff, Paul F. *Industrial Evolution: Organization, Structure, and Growth of the Pennsylvania Iron Industry, 1750–1860.* Baltimore: Johns Hopkins University Press, 1983.

Walker, Joseph E. *Hopewell Village: A Social and Economic History of an Iron-Making Community.* Philadelphia: University of Pennsylvania Press, 1966.

Independence National Historical Park

Independence: A Guide to Independence National Historical Park, Philadelphia, Pennsylvania. Washington: National Park Service, 1982.

Lopez, Claude-Anne, and Eugenia W. Herbert. *The Private Franklin: The Man and His Family.* New York: W. W. Norton, 1975.

Secor, Robert, ed. *Pennsylvania 1776.* University Park: Pennsylvania State University Press, 1975.

Joseph Priestley House

Gibbs, F. W. *Joseph Priestley: Revolutions*

of the Eighteenth Century. Garden City, N.Y.: Doubleday, 1967.

Holt, Anne. A Life of Joseph Priestley. London: Oxford University Press, 1931.

Kieft, Lester and Bennett R. Willeford, eds. Joseph Priestley: Scientist, Theologian and Metaphysician. Lewisburg, Pa.: Bucknell University Press, 1979.

Landis Valley Museum

Jensen, Joan M. Loosening the Bonds: Mid-Atlantic Farm Women, 1750–1850. New Haven: Yale University Press, 1987.

Long, Amos, Jr. The Pennsylvania German Family Farm. Breinigsville: Pennsylvania German Society, 1972.

Swank, Scott T., et al. Arts of the Pennsylvania Germans. New York: W. W. Norton, 1983.

Morton Homestead

Siokalo, Zorianna E., et al. Before Penn: Swedish Colonists in the Land of the Lenape. Philadelphia: American Swedish Historical Society, 1988.

Weslager, C. A. New Sweden on the Delaware, 1638–1655. Wilmington: Middle Atlantic Press, 1988.

Weslager, C. A. The Log Cabin in America, from Pioneer Days to the Present. New Brunswick, N.J.: Rutgers University Press, 1969.

Museum of Anthracite Mining

Binder, Frederick M. Coal Age Empire: Pennsylvania Coal and Its Utilization to 1860. Harrisburg: Pennsylvania Historical and Museum Commission, 1974.

Hudson Coal Company. The Story of Anthracite. New York: The Company, 1932.

Roberts, Ellis W. The Breaker Whistle Blows: Mining Disasters and Labor Leaders in the Anthracite Region. Scranton: Anthracite Museum Press, 1984.

Old Economy Village

Arndt, Karl J. R. George Rapp's Harmony Society, 1785–1847, and George Rapp's Successors and Material Heirs, 1847–1916. Cranbury, N.J.: Associated University Presses, 1972.

Oved, Yaacov. Two Hundred Years of American Communes. New Brunswick, N.J.: Transaction Books, 1986.

Wetzel, Richard D. Frontier Musicians on the Connoquenessing, Wabash and Ohio: A History of the Music and Musicians of George Rapp's Harmony Society (1805–1906). Athens: Ohio University Press, 1976.

Pennsbury Manor

Endy, Melvin B., Jr. William Penn and Early Quakerism. Princeton: Princeton University Press, 1973.

Levy, Barry. Quakers and the American Family: British Settlement in the Delaware Valley. New York: Oxford University Press, 1988.

Peare, Catherine Owens. William Penn: A Biography. Philadelphia: J. B. Lippincott, 1957.

Pennsylvania Anthracite Heritage Museum

Bodnar, John. The Transplanted: A History of Immigrants in Urban America. Bloomington: Indiana University Press, 1985.

Greene, Victor R. The Slavic Community on Strike: Immigrant Labor in Pennsylvania Anthracite. Notre Dame: University of Notre Dame Press, 1968.

Salay, David L. ed. Hard Coal, Hard Times: Ethnicity and Labor in the Anthracite Region. Scranton: Anthracite Museum Press, 1984.

Pennsylvania Lumber Museum

Pinkett, Harold T. Gifford Pinchot, Private and Public Forester. Urbana: University of Illinois Press, 1970.

Taber, Thomas T. Ghost Lumber Towns of Central Pennsylvania. Williamsport, Pa.: Lycoming Printing Co., Inc., 1970.

Tonkin, R. Dudley. My Partner, the River: The White Pine Story on the Susquehanna. Pittsburgh: University of Pittsburgh Press, 1958.

Pennsylvania Military Museum

Ent, Uzal W. The First Century: A History of the 28th Infantry Division. Harrisburg: 28th Infantry Division, 1979.

Jackson, John W. The Pennsylvania Navy, 1775–1781: The Defense of the Delaware. New Brunswick, N.J.: Rutgers University Press, 1974.

Trussell, John B. B. The Commonwealth in Arms: A Guide to Military Sites and Museums in Pennsylvania. Harrisburg: Pennsylvania Historical and Museum Commission, 1987. 48 pp.

Pottsgrove Manor

Andrews, Wayne. Architecture, Ambition, and Americans: A Social History of American Architecture. New York: Free Press, 1978.

Bridenbaugh, Carl and Jessica. Rebels and Gentlemen: Philadelphia in the Age of Franklin. New York: Oxford University Press, 1962.

McCurdy, Linda. The Potts Family Iron Industry in the Schuylkill Valley. Pottstown, Pa.: Pottstown Historical Society, 1975.

Railroad Museum of Pennsylvania

Alexander, Edwin P. On the Main Line: The Pennsylvania Railroad in the 19th Century. New York: Clarkson N. Potter, 1971.

Archer, Robert F. The History of the Lehigh Valley Railroad: The Route of the Black Diamond. Berkeley, Calif.: Howell-North Books, 1977.

Saunders, Richard. The Railroad Mergers and the Coming of Conrail. Westport, Conn.: Greenwood Press, 1978.

Scranton Iron Furnaces

Davies, Edward J. II. The Anthracite Aristocracy: Leadership and Social Change in the Hard Coal Regions of Northeastern Pennsylvania. DeKalb: Northern Illinois University Press, 1985.

Hanlon, Edward F. The Wyoming Valley: An American Portrait. Woodland Hills, Calif.: Windsor Publications, 1983.

Temin, Peter. Iron and Steel in Nineteenth-Century America: An Economic Inquiry. Cambridge: MIT Press, 1964.

Somerset Historical Center

Buck, Solon J. and Elizabeth H. The Planting of Civilization in Western Pennsylvania. Pittsburgh: University of Pittsburgh Press, 1965.

Fletcher, Stevenson W. Pennsylvania Agriculture and Country Life, 1640–1840 and 1840–1940. Harrisburg: Pennsylvania Historical and Museum Commission, 1950 and 1955.

Slaughter, Thomas P. The Whiskey Rebellion: Frontier Epilogue to the American Revolution. New York: Oxford University Press, 1986.

The State Museum of Pennsylvania

Hawke, David Freeman. Nuts and Bolts of the Past: A History of American Technology, 1776–1860. New York: Harper & Row, 1988.

Kent, Barry C. Discovering Pennsylvania's Archeological Heritage. Harrisburg: Pennsylvania Historical and Museum Commission, 1980. 46 pp.

Kricher, John C. A Field Guide to Eastern Forests, North America. (The Peterson Field Guide Series) Boston: Houghton Mifflin, 1988.

Valley Forge National Historical Park

Ketchum, Richard M. The Winter Soldiers. Garden City, N.Y.: Doubleday, 1973.

Royster, Charles. A Revolutionary People at War: The Continental Army and American Character, 1775–1783. Chapel Hill: University of North Carolina Press, 1979.

Trussell, John B. B. Epic on the Schuylkill: The Valley Forge Encampment. Harrisburg: Pennsylvania Historical and Museum Commission, 1986.

Washington Crossing Historic Park

Hutton, Ann Hawkes. Portrait of Patriotism: Washington Crossing the Delaware. Radnor, Pa.: Chilton, 1983.

Smith, Samuel S. The Battle of Princeton. Monmouth Beach, N.J.: Philip Freneau Press, 1967.

Smith, Samuel S. The Battle of Trenton. Monmouth Beach, N.J.: Philip Freneau Press, 1965.

About the Author

Ruth Hoover Seitz was born in Lancaster County, Pennsylvania, on a family farm originally deeded by William Penn's son Thomas. She grew up near Pottsville in the state's anthracite region.

Seitz is the author of the book *Amish Country* and more than 300 published magazine articles. She has traveled extensively in Africa and Asia as a writer for UNICEF and the World Health Organization, and has served as a correspondent for several European magazines.

About the Photographer

Blair Seitz, Ruth's husband, is an editorial and corporate photographer whose work has appeared in *Time, Newsweek, The New York Times Magazine* and European newspapers. He was the photographer for *Amish Country,* published in 1987.

Blair and Ruth live in Harrisburg, Pennsylvania, and are the parents of two daughters.